Peace

Discover the Life-Changing Power of Inner Peace: A Comprehensive Guide to Overcoming Anxiety, Stress, and Negativity and Embracing a Fulfilling and Joyful Existence through Proven Self-Help Strategies, Mindfulness Techniques, and Spiritual Practices!

Lance P. Richards

Peace: Discover the Life-Changing Power of Inner Peace: A Comprehensive Guide to Overcoming Anxiety, Stress, and Negativity and Embracing a Fulfilling and Joyful Existence through Proven Self-Help Strategies, Mindfulness Techniques, and Spiritual Practices!

Table of Contents

01: Introduction: What is Inner Peace and Why is it Important?

In our fast-paced and busy lives, inner peace seems like a distant dream that we can never achieve. We are constantly bombarded with stress, anxiety, and negativity, leaving us feeling drained, overwhelmed, and disconnected from our true selves. But what is inner peace, and why is it so important for our overall wellbeing and happiness?

Inner peace is a state of mind characterized by a deep sense of calm, contentment, and harmony. It is a state of being where we are at peace with ourselves, our surroundings, and the world at large. Inner peace is not just the absence of negative emotions or stress but the presence of positive emotions such as love, joy, and gratitude. It is the foundation for a fulfilling and meaningful existence.

The importance of inner peace cannot be overstated. When we are at peace with ourselves, we are better equipped to handle the challenges of life, and we are less likely to be overwhelmed by stress, anxiety, or negativity. Inner peace helps us to cultivate a positive outlook on life, fosters better relationships with others, and enables us to live a more fulfilling and joyful existence.

01: INTRODUCTION: WHAT IS INNER PEACE AND WHY IS IT IMPORTANT?

The benefits of inner peace are numerous and far-reaching. Studies have shown that individuals who experience inner peace are more resilient in the face of adversity, have better immune systems, and are less likely to suffer from depression or anxiety. They also tend to have better relationships with others, experience higher levels of happiness and life satisfaction, and have a greater sense of purpose and meaning in their lives.

Unfortunately, many of us struggle to find inner peace in our daily lives. We are so caught up in the hustle and bustle of modern life that we forget to take the time to nurture our inner selves. We may find ourselves constantly striving for external validation, material possessions, or success, and neglecting our inner needs for rest, reflection, and self-care.

But the good news is that inner peace is not something that is beyond our reach. It is a state of mind that can be cultivated through self-help strategies, mindfulness techniques, and spiritual practices. By making a conscious effort to prioritize our inner wellbeing, we can discover the life-changing power of inner peace and live a more fulfilling and joyful existence.

01: INTRODUCTION: WHAT IS INNER PEACE AND WHY IS IT IMPORTANT?

This comprehensive guide is designed to help you overcome anxiety, stress, and negativity and embrace a fulfilling and joyful existence through proven self-help strategies, mindfulness techniques, and spiritual practices. It will provide you with the tools and knowledge you need to cultivate inner peace and create a life that is filled with purpose, meaning, and happiness.

In the chapters that follow, we will explore various aspects of inner peace, including the causes and effects of stress and anxiety, the benefits of mindfulness and meditation, the importance of self-care and self-compassion, and the role of spirituality in cultivating inner peace. We will also provide practical tips and exercises that you can use to incorporate these practices into your daily life and begin your journey towards inner peace.

So, if you are ready to discover the life-changing power of inner peace, then let's get started!

02: The Connection between Inner Peace and Mental Health

The human mind is a complex and intricate system that controls our every thought, feeling, and action. Our mental health plays a crucial role in shaping our lives and determining our overall well-being. Mental health issues can arise due to various factors, including genetics, environment, lifestyle, and personal experiences. Anxiety, depression, stress, and negativity are some common mental health challenges that many people face in their lives.

Inner peace is a state of being that is characterized by a sense of calm, contentment, and harmony. It is a state of mind that is free from worry, anxiety, and negative thoughts. Inner peace is not something that can be achieved overnight. It requires effort, commitment, and practice. However, the benefits of achieving inner peace are immense. Inner peace can help to reduce stress, anxiety, and negative emotions, leading to improved mental health.

Studies have shown that there is a strong connection between inner peace and mental health. People who are able to achieve a state of inner peace are more likely to have better mental health and well-being. Inner peace helps to reduce stress and anxiety, which are two of the most common mental health challenges that people face. When we are stressed or anxious, our body produces cortisol, a hormone that can have negative effects on our mental and physical health. Inner peace helps to reduce the production of cortisol, leading to improved mental health.

Inner peace can also help to improve our overall mood and emotional well-being. When we are in a state of inner peace, we are more likely to experience positive emotions such as joy, gratitude, and love. These positive emotions can have a profound effect on our mental health, helping to reduce anxiety and depression.

Practicing mindfulness is one effective way to achieve inner peace and improve mental health. Mindfulness involves being present in the moment and paying attention to our thoughts, feelings, and sensations without judgment. When we practice mindfulness, we are able to observe our thoughts and emotions without getting caught up in them. This helps to reduce stress and anxiety and improve our overall mental health.

Spiritual practices such as meditation, prayer, and yoga can also help to achieve inner peace and improve mental health. These practices help to quiet the mind and promote a sense of calm and relaxation. They also help to cultivate feelings of gratitude, compassion, and love, which can have a positive effect on our mental health.

In addition to mindfulness and spiritual practices, there are several self-help strategies that can help to achieve inner peace and improve mental health. These strategies include:

Self-care: Taking care of ourselves physically, emotionally, and mentally is crucial for achieving inner peace and improving mental health. This includes getting enough sleep, eating a healthy diet, exercising regularly, and engaging in activities that bring us joy and fulfillment.

Positive self-talk: Our thoughts can have a powerful impact on our mental health. Positive self-talk involves replacing negative thoughts with positive ones. This can help to reduce stress and anxiety and improve our overall mood.

Gratitude: Practicing gratitude involves focusing on the positive aspects of our lives and expressing gratitude for them. This can help to cultivate feelings of joy and contentment, leading to improved mental health.

Social support: Having a strong support system can help to reduce stress and anxiety and improve mental health. This includes friends, family, and other supportive individuals who we can turn to for help and encouragement.

In conclusion, achieving inner peace is a powerful tool for improving mental health. Inner peace helps to reduce stress, anxiety, and negative emotions, leading to improved mental and physical health. Mindfulness, spiritual practices, and self-help strategies can all help to achieve inner peace and improve mental health. By making inner peace a priority in our lives, we can experience a more fulfilling and joyful existence.

03: Understanding Anxiety and Stress: Causes, Symptoms, and Effects

Anxiety and stress are common emotions experienced by everyone at some point in their lives. They are natural responses to challenging situations, which can have both positive and negative effects. However, when these emotions become excessive and interfere with daily life, they can lead to serious physical and mental health problems. In this chapter, we will delve deeper into understanding anxiety and stress, their causes, symptoms, and effects.

Understanding Anxiety

Anxiety is a feeling of unease or worry about future events or situations. It is a normal human emotion that can be helpful in certain situations, such as preparing for a test, interview, or public speaking. However, excessive anxiety can become a disorder that affects one's mental and physical health.

Causes of Anxiety

Anxiety can have various causes, including genetic, environmental, and psychological factors. Some of the common causes of anxiety include:

– Genetics: People with a family history of anxiety disorders are more likely to experience anxiety themselves.

– Trauma: Experiencing a traumatic event such as abuse, violence, or natural disasters can trigger anxiety disorders.

– Stress: Chronic stress from work, relationships, financial problems, or health issues can lead to anxiety disorders.

– Brain chemistry: Changes in brain chemistry, particularly in the levels of neurotransmitters such as serotonin and dopamine, can lead to anxiety.

Symptoms of Anxiety

The symptoms of anxiety can vary from person to person and can be physical, emotional, and behavioral. Some of the common symptoms of anxiety include:

– Physical symptoms: Sweating, trembling, racing heartbeat, chest pain, shortness of breath, nausea, and gastrointestinal problems.

– Emotional symptoms: Feeling worried, fearful, apprehensive, and restless.

– Behavioral symptoms: Avoiding situations or activities that trigger anxiety, seeking reassurance from others, and compulsive behaviors such as checking, cleaning, or counting.

Effects of Anxiety

Untreated anxiety can have significant negative effects on one's physical and mental health. Some of the effects of anxiety include:

– Depression: Chronic anxiety can lead to depression and vice versa.

– Substance abuse: People with anxiety disorders are more likely to abuse drugs or alcohol as a way of coping with their symptoms.

– Physical health problems: Chronic anxiety can lead to high blood pressure, heart disease, and other physical health problems.

— Impaired social functioning: Anxiety can affect one's ability to interact with others, form relationships, and perform well in social situations.

Understanding Stress

Stress is the body's natural response to demands or threats. It is a necessary and normal part of life that helps us cope with challenging situations. However, chronic or excessive stress can lead to physical and mental health problems.

Causes of Stress

Stress can be caused by various factors, including:

— Work-related stress: Pressure at work, long working hours, and job insecurity can lead to stress.

— Financial stress: Money problems, debt, and financial insecurity can cause stress.

— Relationship stress: Problems in relationships with partners, family, or friends can lead to stress.

— Health-related stress: Chronic illness, disability, or caring for a sick family member can cause stress.

Symptoms of Stress

The symptoms of stress can vary from person to person and can be physical, emotional, and behavioral. Some of the common symptoms of stress include:

– Physical symptoms: Headaches, muscle tension, fatigue, and sleep problems.

– Emotional symptoms: Feeling overwhelmed, irritable, anxious, and moody.

– Behavioral symptoms: Procrastination, social withdrawal, and unhealthy coping mechanisms such as overeating, smoking, or drinking.

Effects of Stress

Chronic stress can have significant negative effects on one's physical and mental health. Some of the effects of stress include:

– Mental health problems: Chronic stress can lead to anxiety, depression, and other mental health disorders.

– Physical health problems: Chronic stress can weaken the immune system, increase the risk of heart disease, and cause digestive problems.

– Relationship problems: Chronic stress can lead to conflicts in relationships and affect one's ability to form new relationships.

– Occupational problems: Chronic stress can lead to decreased productivity, absenteeism, and burnout.

Managing Anxiety and Stress

Managing anxiety and stress is essential for maintaining a healthy and fulfilling life. There are various self-help strategies, mindfulness techniques, and spiritual practices that can help manage anxiety and stress. Some of these strategies include:

– Exercise: Regular physical exercise, such as jogging, swimming, or yoga, can reduce stress and anxiety and improve overall mental and physical health.

– Mindfulness meditation: Practicing mindfulness meditation can help reduce anxiety and stress by increasing awareness of the present moment.

– Relaxation techniques: Deep breathing exercises, progressive muscle relaxation, and visualization can help reduce anxiety and stress.

– Self-care: Taking care of oneself through healthy eating, getting enough sleep, and engaging in pleasurable activities can help reduce stress and anxiety.

– Social support: Seeking support from family, friends, or a therapist can help reduce stress and anxiety and improve overall mental health.

Conclusion

Anxiety and stress are common emotions experienced by everyone. While they can be helpful in certain situations, excessive anxiety and stress can lead to significant negative effects on one's physical and mental health. Understanding the causes, symptoms, and effects of anxiety and stress is essential for managing them effectively. There are various

03: UNDERSTANDING ANXIETY AND STRESS: CAUSES, SYMPTOMS, AND EFFECTS

self-help strategies, mindfulness techniques, and spiritual practices that can help manage anxiety and stress and lead to a more fulfilling and joyful existence.

04: Breaking Free from Negative Thought Patterns

Introduction:

Negative thought patterns are an inevitable part of the human experience. Whether it's a passing negative thought or a persistent negative belief, these patterns can wreak havoc on our mental, emotional, and physical well-being. The good news is that negative thought patterns are not permanent, and we have the power to change them. In this chapter, we will explore the nature of negative thought patterns, their impact on our lives, and strategies for breaking free from them.

Understanding Negative Thought Patterns:

Negative thought patterns are habitual ways of thinking that are pessimistic, self-defeating, and limiting. These patterns are often automatic, and we may not even be aware of them. They can be triggered by external events, internal dialogue, or past experiences. Examples of negative thought patterns include:

– Catastrophizing: Assuming the worst possible outcome of

04: BREAKING FREE FROM NEGATIVE THOUGHT PAT-TERNS

a situation

– All-or-nothing thinking: Seeing things in black and white terms, with no room for gray areas

– Overgeneralizing: Making sweeping conclusions based on one or two experiences

– Personalization: Blaming oneself for events outside of one's control

The Impact of Negative Thought Patterns:

Negative thought patterns can have a profound impact on our lives. They can lead to anxiety, depression, low self-esteem, and other mental health issues. They can also affect our relationships, work, and overall quality of life. Negative thought patterns can create a self-fulfilling prophecy, where we believe something negative will happen, and then act in ways that make it more likely to occur.

Breaking Free from Negative Thought Patterns:

Breaking free from negative thought patterns takes time, effort, and commitment. It requires self-awareness, self-compassion, and a willingness to change. Here are some strategies for breaking free from negative thought patterns:

Identify Your Negative Thought Patterns:

The first step in breaking free from negative thought patterns is to identify them. Start by paying attention to your thoughts throughout the day. Notice when negative thoughts arise and write them down. Once you have a list of negative thought patterns, you can begin to challenge them.

Challenge Your Negative Thought Patterns:

Negative thought patterns are often based on cognitive distortions, which are errors in thinking. By challenging these distortions, you can begin to break free from negative thought patterns. Ask yourself questions such as:

– Is this thought true?

– Is there evidence to support this thought?

– Is this thought helpful or harmful?

– What would I say to a friend who had this thought?

04: BREAKING FREE FROM NEGATIVE THOUGHT PAT-
TERNS

By questioning your negative thoughts, you can begin to see them in a more balanced and realistic way.

Practice Self-Compassion:

Negative thought patterns can be self-critical and judg-mental. Practicing self-compassion involves treating your-self with kindness, understanding, and forgiveness. When you have a negative thought, try to respond to yourself as you would to a friend. Offer yourself words of encourage-ment and support.

Cultivate Positive Thought Patterns:

Breaking free from negative thought patterns involves not only challenging them but also replacing them with positive thought patterns. Focus on what is going well in your life, your strengths, and your accomplishments. Practice gratit-ude and appreciation for the good things in your life.

Practice Mindfulness:

Mindfulness is the practice of being present and non-judg-mental in the moment. By practicing mindfulness, you can become more aware of your negative thought patterns and learn to observe them without reacting to them. Mindfulness can also help you develop a sense of inner peace and calm.

Seek Professional Help:

Breaking free from negative thought patterns can be challenging, and sometimes it requires professional help. Consider seeking the guidance of a therapist or counselor who can help you identify and challenge your negative thought patterns. A mental health professional can also provide support and guidance as you work to break free from negative thought patterns.

Engage in Physical Activity:

Physical activity can be an effective way to break free from negative thought patterns. Exercise releases endorphins, which are natural mood boosters. Physical activity can also distract you from negative thoughts and provide a sense of accomplishment and self-confidence.

Engage in Spiritual Practices:

Engaging in spiritual practices such as meditation, prayer,

or yoga can help you cultivate inner peace and calm. These practices can also help you develop a sense of purpose and meaning in life, which can counteract negative thought patterns.

Conclusion:

Breaking free from negative thought patterns is a process that takes time and effort. It requires self-awareness, self-compassion, and a willingness to change. By identifying your negative thought patterns, challenging them, practicing self-compassion, cultivating positive thought patterns, practicing mindfulness, seeking professional help if needed, engaging in physical activity, and engaging in spiritual practices, you can break free from negative thought patterns and live a more fulfilling and joyful existence. Remember that breaking free from negative thought patterns is not a one-time event but an ongoing process. Be patient with yourself and celebrate your progress along the way.

05: The Science of Happiness: How Inner Peace Can Improve Your Life

In today's fast-paced world, it's easy to get caught up in the hustle and bustle of everyday life. We're constantly bombarded with stimuli from our phones, social media, work, and relationships, leaving us feeling overwhelmed, stressed, and anxious. But what if there was a way to break free from the chaos and experience a sense of peace and contentment, even in the midst of the chaos? Enter the science of happiness.

In recent years, there has been a surge of interest in the study of happiness, with researchers from various fields delving into what makes us happy and how we can cultivate more happiness in our lives. Studies have shown that happiness is not just a fleeting emotion but a state of being that can be cultivated through intentional actions and habits.

So, how does happiness relate to inner peace? Inner peace is a state of calmness and tranquility that arises from within us, regardless of external circumstances. It's a sense of being grounded and centered, even in the midst of chaos.

05: THE SCIENCE OF HAPPINESS: HOW INNER PEACE CAN IMPROVE YOUR LIFE

When we experience inner peace, we're able to navigate life's ups and downs with greater ease and grace, which, in turn, leads to greater happiness.

But how do we cultivate inner peace? There are many self-help strategies, mindfulness techniques, and spiritual practices that can help us tap into this powerful state of being. Let's explore some of them in greater detail.

Self-Help Strategies for Cultivating Inner Peace

Self-help strategies are actions we can take on our own to improve our mental and emotional well-being. Here are some self-help strategies that can help cultivate inner peace:

Prioritize Self-Care: Self-care involves taking care of our physical, emotional, and mental well-being. This can include getting enough sleep, eating a healthy diet, engaging in regular exercise, and taking time to engage in activities that bring us joy.

Practice Gratitude: Gratitude is the practice of intentionally focusing on the positive aspects of our lives and expressing appreciation for them. Gratitude has been shown to improve overall well-being and increase feelings of happiness and contentment.

Set Boundaries: Boundaries are guidelines we set for ourselves and others that help us maintain healthy relationships and protect our emotional well-being. Setting boundaries can help reduce stress and promote a sense of calm.

Practice Mindfulness: Mindfulness involves being fully present in the moment and non-judgmentally observing our thoughts, emotions, and physical sensations. Mindfulness has been shown to reduce stress, increase emotional regulation, and promote overall well-being.

Mindfulness Techniques for Cultivating Inner Peace

Mindfulness techniques are practices that help us cultivate a state of mindfulness. Here are some mindfulness techniques that can help cultivate inner peace:

Meditation: Meditation is a practice of focusing the mind on a specific object or activity, such as the breath or a mantra. Meditation has been shown to reduce stress, increase emotional regulation, and promote overall well-being.

Body Scan: Body scan is a mindfulness technique that involves focusing on different parts of the body and observing physical sensations without judgment. Body scan has been shown to reduce stress and promote a sense of calm.

Walking Meditation: Walking meditation is a mindfulness technique that involves walking slowly and intentionally, focusing on the sensations of each step. Walking meditation has been shown to reduce stress and promote overall well-being.

Spiritual Practices for Cultivating Inner Peace

Spiritual practices involve connecting with a higher power or purpose. Here are some spiritual practices that can help cultivate inner peace:

Prayer: Prayer is a practice of communicating with a higher power or expressing gratitude for blessings. Prayer has been shown to reduce stress and increase feelings of hope and optimism.

Yoga: Yoga is a physical, mental, and spiritual practice that involves stretching, breathing, and mindfulness. Yoga has been shown to reduce stress, improve physical health, and promote overall well-being.

Journaling: Journaling involves reflecting on thoughts, emotions, and experiences in a written format. Journaling has been shown to increase self-awareness, reduce stress, and promote overall well-being.

Service: Service involves helping others and contributing to a greater good. Service has been shown to increase feelings of connection and purpose, reduce stress, and promote overall well-being.

The Benefits of Inner Peace and Happiness

Cultivating inner peace and happiness can have a profound impact on our lives. Here are some of the benefits:

Reduced Stress: Inner peace and happiness can help reduce stress, which has been linked to a variety of physical and mental health problems.

Improved Physical Health: Inner peace and happiness have been linked to improved physical health, including lower blood pressure, improved immune function, and reduced inflammation.

Improved Mental Health: Inner peace and happiness have been linked to improved mental health, including reduced symptoms of anxiety and depression.

Improved Relationships: Inner peace and happiness can improve our relationships by helping us communicate more effectively, show more empathy and compassion, and be more present with others.

Greater Resilience: Inner peace and happiness can help us navigate life's ups and downs with greater ease and grace, increasing our resilience in the face of adversity.

In conclusion, the science of happiness and inner peace offers a wealth of strategies, techniques, and practices that can help us cultivate a more fulfilling and joyful existence. By prioritizing self-care, practicing mindfulness, engaging in spiritual practices, and focusing on gratitude, we can tap into a powerful state of being that can transform our lives in countless ways. Whether you're looking to reduce stress, improve your physical or mental health, or deepen your connections with others, cultivating inner peace and happiness is a powerful way to achieve these goals and live a more fulfilling life.

06: Mindfulness: The Power of Living in the Present Moment

The concept of mindfulness has been around for thousands of years, and it has been used by different cultures and traditions as a way of enhancing wellbeing and inner peace. Mindfulness is the practice of being fully present and engaged in the present moment, without judgment or distraction. It involves paying attention to our thoughts, feelings, and physical sensations in a non-judgmental way, and learning to observe them without reacting or getting caught up in them.

The benefits of mindfulness are numerous and have been scientifically proven. Research shows that practicing mindfulness can reduce stress and anxiety, enhance emotional regulation, improve focus and attention, and even boost the immune system. It is also effective in treating depression, addiction, and other mental health issues.

One of the key principles of mindfulness is acceptance. This means accepting the present moment for what it is, without trying to change it or judge it. This can be a challenge, especially when we are facing difficult situations or emotions. However, by practicing acceptance, we can learn to let go of resistance and allow things to be as they are.

Another important aspect of mindfulness is non-judgment.
When we practice mindfulness, we learn to observe our
thoughts and emotions without attaching labels or judg-
ments to them. This can help us to become more self-aware
and less reactive, and can lead to greater emotional regulation and inner peace.

Mindfulness can be practiced in many different ways, including through meditation, yoga, and other forms of mindful movement. One of the most common mindfulness practices is breath awareness. This involves focusing our attention on our breath, observing the sensations of the breath as
it moves in and out of our body, and bringing our attention
back to the breath whenever our mind wanders.

Body scan meditation is another mindfulness practice that
involves systematically scanning the body for sensations
and observing them without judgment. This can be a powerful tool for becoming more aware of our physical sensations
and learning to connect with our bodies in a deeper way.

Mindful movement practices, such as yoga or tai chi, involve paying attention to the movements of the body and the sensations they create, as well as the breath. These practices can be particularly helpful for those who find it difficult to sit still for extended periods of time.

In addition to these formal mindfulness practices, we can also incorporate mindfulness into our daily lives by bringing awareness to our activities and interactions. This can involve being fully present and engaged in our conversations with others, paying attention to the sights and sounds around us as we go about our day, and even bringing awareness to the sensations of our feet as we walk.

The practice of mindfulness is not always easy, and it can be particularly challenging in our fast-paced and often distracting world. However, with practice and persistence, we can learn to cultivate greater awareness, acceptance, and inner peace in our lives. By embracing the present moment and learning to observe our thoughts and emotions without judgment, we can discover the life-changing power of mindfulness and unlock a deeper sense of joy and fulfillment.

07: Practicing Gratitude: Finding Joy in Everyday Life

Gratitude is a powerful force that can transform our lives. When we practice gratitude, we shift our focus from what we lack to what we have. We begin to appreciate the good things in our lives and we become more open to new opportunities and experiences. In this chapter, we will explore the benefits of practicing gratitude and discover how to cultivate a grateful mindset.

The Benefits of Practicing Gratitude

Gratitude has numerous benefits for our mental and physical health. Research has shown that people who practice gratitude are happier, less stressed, and more resilient. They also have stronger social connections and are more satisfied with their lives.

One of the main benefits of gratitude is that it helps us focus on the positive aspects of our lives. When we are grateful, we are less likely to dwell on negative thoughts and emotions. Instead, we are able to appreciate the good things in our lives and find joy in everyday experiences.

Gratitude can also improve our relationships with others. When we express gratitude to those around us, we strengthen our bonds and create a positive cycle of giving and receiving. Gratitude can also help us forgive others and let go of negative emotions that can harm our relationships.

Finally, gratitude has physical benefits as well. Studies have shown that people who practice gratitude have lower levels of stress hormones and better immune function. Gratitude can also improve sleep quality and reduce symptoms of depression and anxiety.

Cultivating a Grateful Mindset

So how can we cultivate a grateful mindset? Here are some strategies to get started:

Keep a gratitude journal. Writing down things you are grateful for each day can help you focus on the positive aspects of your life. Try to write down at least three things each day, no matter how small.

Practice mindfulness. When we are mindful, we are more aware of the present moment and can appreciate the beauty around us. Try taking a few moments each day to focus on your breath or your surroundings.

Express gratitude to others. When we express gratitude to others, we not only make them feel good, but we also strengthen our own relationships. Try thanking someone each day for something they have done for you.

Reframe negative experiences. When something negative happens, try to find a positive aspect to focus on. For example, if you get stuck in traffic, use the time to listen to a podcast or enjoy the scenery.

Volunteer or give back. Helping others can be a great way to cultivate gratitude and perspective. Consider volunteering at a local charity or donating to a cause you care about.

Practice self-compassion. Being kind to ourselves can help us appreciate the good things in our lives. Try to treat yourself with the same kindness and understanding you would show a close friend.

Incorporating Gratitude into Your Daily Life

Once you have begun to cultivate a grateful mindset, it is

important to continue practicing gratitude in your daily life. Here are some tips for incorporating gratitude into your routine:

Start each day with gratitude. Before you even get out of bed, take a moment to reflect on something you are grateful for.

Use gratitude as a coping mechanism. When you are feeling stressed or overwhelmed, take a few moments to focus on what you are grateful for. This can help shift your mindset and reduce negative emotions.

Create gratitude rituals. Consider creating a gratitude ritual, such as writing in your gratitude journal before bed or expressing gratitude before meals.

Surround yourself with gratitude. Surrounding yourself with reminders of what you are grateful for can help reinforce your grateful mindset. Consider placing inspiring quotes or images around your home or office.

Share your gratitude with others. When you express gratitude to others, you not only strengthen your own relationships but also inspire others to practice gratitude.

Conclusion

Practicing gratitude can transform our lives in numerous ways. By focusing on the positive aspects of our lives and appreciating the good things, we can experience greater happiness, reduce stress and anxiety, improve our relationships with others, and even improve our physical health.

Cultivating a grateful mindset takes practice and effort, but the benefits are well worth it. By incorporating gratitude into our daily lives, we can create a more joyful and fulfilling existence.

Remember, gratitude is not just about being thankful for the big things in life. It is about finding joy in the small moments and appreciating the beauty that surrounds us every day. So take a moment to look around and appreciate the people, experiences, and things that bring you joy and make your life richer. By doing so, you can tap into the life-changing power of gratitude and discover the true meaning of inner peace.

08: The Benefits of Meditation: Cultivating Inner Calm and Clarity

Meditation has been practiced for thousands of years in various cultures and traditions around the world. It is a technique that involves training the mind to focus and attain a state of relaxation and clarity. Meditation has numerous benefits for our mental and physical health and has been proven to be an effective way to manage stress, anxiety, and negativity. In this chapter, we will explore the benefits of meditation and how it can help cultivate inner calm and clarity.

Reduces Stress and Anxiety:

Stress and anxiety are a part of everyday life, and they can have a significant impact on our mental and physical health. Meditation has been shown to reduce the levels of stress hormones in the body, such as cortisol and adrenaline. By reducing the levels of stress hormones, meditation can help alleviate symptoms of anxiety and promote feelings of calm and relaxation.

Improves Sleep Quality:

08: THE BENEFITS OF MEDITATION: CULTIVATING IN-NER CALM AND CLARITY

Meditation has been found to improve the quality of sleep by reducing the amount of time it takes to fall asleep and decreasing the number of nighttime awakenings. It can also help reduce symptoms of insomnia, such as difficulty falling asleep or staying asleep.

Enhances Emotional Well-being:

Meditation has been shown to enhance emotional well-being by reducing symptoms of depression, anger, and negativity. It can also improve feelings of happiness, positivity, and overall satisfaction with life.

Boosts Focus and Concentration:

Meditation helps to train the mind to focus and concentrate on the present moment. By practicing meditation regularly, you can improve your ability to focus and concentrate, making it easier to complete tasks and improve productivity.

Increases Self-awareness:

Meditation helps to cultivate self-awareness by allowing you to observe your thoughts and feelings without judgment. By becoming more aware of your thoughts and emotions, you can develop a deeper understanding of yourself and your inner world.

Promotes Physical Health:

Meditation has been found to have numerous physical health benefits, such as reducing blood pressure, improving immune function, and reducing inflammation in the body. It can also help alleviate symptoms of chronic pain and improve overall physical well-being.

Enhances Creativity:

Meditation has been shown to enhance creativity by allowing the mind to access new ideas and ways of thinking. By quieting the mind and reducing distractions, meditation can help tap into the creative potential of the mind.

Cultivates Compassion and Empathy:

Meditation has been found to cultivate compassion and empathy by reducing negative emotions and increasing feelings of love, kindness, and empathy towards oneself and others.

08: THE BENEFITS OF MEDITATION: CULTIVATING IN-NER CALM AND CLARITY

Increases Resilience:

Meditation can help increase resilience by providing a sense of calm and inner strength during difficult times. By cultivating inner calm and clarity through meditation, you can better navigate the challenges of life and bounce back from adversity.

Promotes Spiritual Growth:

Meditation is often used as a spiritual practice in various religious and spiritual traditions. It can help cultivate a deeper sense of connection with oneself and the universe, promoting spiritual growth and a sense of purpose in life.

In conclusion, meditation has numerous benefits for our mental and physical health and can help cultivate inner calm and clarity. By practicing meditation regularly, you can improve your overall well-being and develop a deeper sense of self-awareness and connection with yourself and the world around you. So, if you're looking for a way to manage stress, anxiety, and negativity, or simply want to improve your overall well-being, consider incorporating meditation into your daily routine.

09: Yoga and Inner Peace: Connecting Mind, Body, and Spirit

Yoga is an ancient practice that has been around for over 5,000 years. It originated in India and has since spread throughout the world, becoming a popular form of exercise, meditation, and spiritual practice. Yoga is a Sanskrit word that means "union" or "connection." The practice of yoga involves connecting the mind, body, and spirit through a series of physical postures, breathing exercises, and meditation techniques.

The physical postures of yoga, called asanas, are designed to improve flexibility, strength, and balance. Each posture has its own unique benefits, and when practiced together in a sequence, they can create a sense of harmony and flow in the body. Asanas can also help to relieve tension and stress, and can improve circulation and digestion.

Breathing exercises, called pranayama, are an important part of the yoga practice. These exercises help to regulate the breath and bring awareness to the present moment. By focusing on the breath, practitioners can calm the mind and reduce feelings of anxiety and stress. Pranayama can also improve lung capacity and oxygenation of the blood.

Meditation is another key component of yoga. It involves sitting in stillness and focusing the mind on a particular object, sound, or sensation. Meditation can help to quiet the mind, reduce negative thoughts, and promote feelings of relaxation and inner peace. Regular meditation practice has been shown to have numerous health benefits, including reducing symptoms of depression and anxiety, improving sleep quality, and lowering blood pressure.

Yoga is not just a physical practice, but also a spiritual one. The practice of yoga encourages practitioners to connect with their inner selves and to cultivate a sense of mindfulness and self-awareness. Through regular practice, practitioners can develop a deeper understanding of themselves and their place in the world. They may also experience a greater sense of connection to others and to the universe as a whole.

One of the key benefits of yoga is its ability to promote inner peace. By connecting the mind, body, and spirit, yoga can help to quiet the mind and reduce feelings of stress and anxiety. This can lead to a greater sense of calm and well-being, and can help practitioners to navigate life's challenges with greater ease and resilience.

In addition to its physical and spiritual benefits, yoga has also been shown to have numerous health benefits. Studies have found that regular yoga practice can improve cardiovascular health, reduce chronic pain, and even improve cognitive function. Yoga has also been shown to be an effective treatment for a variety of mental health conditions, including depression, anxiety, and post-traumatic stress disorder (PTSD).

There are many different styles of yoga, each with its own unique emphasis and approach. Some styles, such as Hatha and Vinyasa, are more physically demanding, while others, such as Yin and Restorative, are more gentle and focused on relaxation. Some styles, such as Kundalini and Ashtanga, incorporate more spiritual elements and meditation practices.

Regardless of the style, however, the practice of yoga can be a powerful tool for promoting inner peace and wellbeing. Whether practiced in a studio, at home, or in nature, yoga offers a way to connect with the present moment and to cultivate a sense of mindfulness and self-awareness. By incorporating yoga into your daily routine, you can tap into the life-changing power of inner peace and embrace a more fulfilling and joyful existence.

10: The Art of Deep Relaxation: Restoring Balance and Harmony

Introduction

In today's fast-paced world, it's not uncommon to feel over-whelmed and stressed out. Many people find themselves struggling to keep up with the demands of their busy lives, leaving them feeling depleted, anxious, and even depressed. The good news is that there are proven techniques you can use to restore balance and harmony in your life. In this chapter, we'll explore the art of deep relaxation, which can help you overcome anxiety, stress, and negativity and embrace a fulfilling and joyful existence.

The Importance of Deep Relaxation

Before we dive into the techniques of deep relaxation, let's first explore why it's so important. When we're stressed, our bodies go into fight-or-flight mode, which can be helpful in short bursts but can cause long-term harm if sustained. Chronic stress can lead to a variety of health problems, including high blood pressure, heart disease, and obesity.

Deep relaxation, on the other hand, triggers the relaxation

response, which can counteract the harmful effects of stress. When you're in a state of deep relaxation, your heart rate slows, your muscles relax, and your breathing becomes deeper and more regular. This state of deep relaxation can help reduce anxiety and improve your overall sense of well-being.

Techniques for Deep Relaxation

There are many techniques you can use to achieve a state of deep relaxation. Here are some of the most effective:

Progressive Muscle Relaxation

Progressive muscle relaxation involves tensing and then relaxing each muscle group in your body, one at a time. This technique can help release physical tension and promote relaxation. To practice progressive muscle relaxation, lie down in a quiet, comfortable place and follow these steps:

– Start with your toes and tense them for a few seconds, then release.

– Move up to your feet and do the same thing.

– Continue working your way up your body, tensing and then relaxing each muscle group, including your calves, thighs, buttocks, abdomen, chest, back, arms, and face.

Visualization

Visualization is a powerful tool that can help you relax and reduce stress. To practice visualization, find a quiet, comfortable place to sit or lie down and follow these steps:

– Close your eyes and imagine a peaceful scene, such as a beach, a forest, or a mountain.

– Try to engage all your senses in the visualization. For example, if you're imagining a beach, picture the waves lapping at the shore, feel the warmth of the sun on your skin, and hear the sound of seagulls.

– Stay with the visualization for several minutes, allowing yourself to fully immerse in the scene.

Breathing Techniques

Breathing techniques can help slow your heart rate, calm your mind, and promote relaxation. Here are two effective breathing techniques:

– Diaphragmatic Breathing: To practice diaphragmatic breathing, sit or lie down and place one hand on your chest and the other on your belly. Take a deep breath in through your nose, and feel your belly rise. Exhale slowly through your mouth, and feel your belly fall. Repeat for several minutes.

– 4-7-8 Breathing: To practice 4-7-8 breathing, sit or lie down and follow these steps:

– Exhale completely through your mouth.

– Close your mouth and inhale through your nose for a count of 4.

– Hold your breath for a count of 7.

– Exhale through your mouth for a count of 8.

– Repeat the cycle for several minutes.

Mindfulness Meditation

Mindfulness meditation is a powerful technique that can

help you stay present in the moment and reduce stress. To practice mindfulness meditation, find a quiet, comfortable place to sit and follow these steps:

– Close your eyes and focus your attention on your breath.

– Notice the sensation of the air moving in and out of your body.

– If your mind starts to wander, gently bring it back to your breath.

– Try to stay present in the moment, without judgment or distraction.

Yoga

Yoga is a holistic practice that combines physical postures with breath control and meditation. Practicing yoga can help reduce stress, improve flexibility and strength, and promote relaxation. There are many different styles of yoga, so find one that resonates with you and start practicing regularly.

Incorporating Deep Relaxation into Your Daily Routine

10: THE ART OF DEEP RELAXATION: RESTORING BAL-ANCE AND HARMONY

Now that you've learned some effective techniques for deep relaxation, it's time to start incorporating them into your daily routine. Here are some tips to help you get started:

Schedule Time for Relaxation

Make relaxation a priority by scheduling time for it each day. Even if it's just a few minutes, setting aside time for relaxation can help make it a habit.

Create a Relaxing Environment

Find a quiet, comfortable place where you can practice deep relaxation without distraction. Dim the lights, light a candle or some incense, and play some soothing music to create a calming environment.

Practice Consistently

To see the benefits of deep relaxation, it's important to practice consistently. Start by setting aside 5-10 minutes each day, and gradually increase the time as you become more comfortable with the techniques.

Be Patient

10: THE ART OF DEEP RELAXATION: RESTORING BALANCE AND HARMONY

Deep relaxation takes practice, so be patient with yourself. It may take time to find the techniques that work best for you, but with persistence and patience, you can achieve a state of deep relaxation.

Conclusion

Deep relaxation is a powerful tool that can help you overcome anxiety, stress, and negativity and embrace a fulfilling and joyful existence. By practicing techniques like progressive muscle relaxation, visualization, breathing techniques, mindfulness meditation, and yoga, you can trigger the relaxation response and promote a sense of calm and balance in your life. Remember to be patient, consistent, and gentle with yourself as you explore the art of deep relaxation. With practice and persistence, you can achieve a state of deep relaxation and experience the life-changing power of inner peace.

11: The Healing Power of Nature: Connecting with the Natural World

Nature has always been a source of inspiration and healing for humanity. From the majestic mountains to the calmness of a lake, the natural world has a way of rejuvenating our souls and refreshing our minds. In this chapter, we will explore the healing power of nature and how connecting with the natural world can bring inner peace, reduce stress, and promote well-being.

There is no denying that our modern lifestyles have made it difficult to connect with nature. We spend most of our time indoors, surrounded by screens and artificial lights, disconnected from the natural rhythms of the world. This disconnection has led to a rise in stress, anxiety, and other mental health issues. However, studies have shown that spending time in nature can have a profound impact on our mental and physical health.

One of the ways that nature can help us find inner peace is by providing us with a sense of awe and wonder. When we see the beauty of a sunset or the majesty of a mountain, we are reminded that we are part of something greater than ourselves. This sense of awe can help us put our problems into perspective and give us a greater sense of purpose and meaning.

In addition to awe, nature also provides us with a sense of tranquility and calmness. When we are surrounded by the natural world, we can feel our stress levels decrease, and our bodies relax. Studies have shown that spending time in nature can lower cortisol levels, which is a hormone associated with stress. This reduction in stress can lead to a variety of benefits, including improved immune function, better sleep, and reduced inflammation.

Furthermore, nature can help us cultivate mindfulness, which is a key component of inner peace. When we are in nature, we are forced to slow down and pay attention to the present moment. We become more aware of our senses and our surroundings, which can help us become more mindful and present in our daily lives. This mindfulness can help us reduce our negative thoughts and feelings, allowing us to find greater peace and happiness.

So, how can we connect with nature and experience its healing power? There are many ways to do so, and the best way will depend on your personal preferences and circumstances. Here are some ideas to get you started:

Take a walk in the park: This is a simple and easy way to connect with nature, and it can be done almost anywhere. Whether it's a local park or a national forest, taking a walk in nature can help you clear your mind and reduce stress.

Go camping: Spending a few days camping in the wilderness can be a transformative experience. It allows you to disconnect from the distractions of daily life and connect with the natural world on a deeper level.

Practice yoga outside: Yoga is a great way to cultivate mindfulness and inner peace, and practicing outside can enhance the experience. Whether it's in a park or on a beach, doing yoga outside can help you connect with nature and find inner peace.

Meditate in nature: Meditating outside can be a powerful way to cultivate mindfulness and inner peace. Find a quiet spot in nature, sit down, and focus on your breath. Allow the sounds and sensations of nature to wash over you and bring you into a state of calmness.

Volunteer in nature: Volunteering in nature can be a rewarding way to connect with the natural world while also giving back to your community. Whether it's planting trees or cleaning up a beach, volunteering in nature can be a powerful way to find purpose and meaning.

In conclusion, nature has a profound healing power that can help us find inner peace, reduce stress, and promote well-being. By connecting with the natural world, we can cultivate awe, tranquility, and mindfulness, allowing us to find greater peace and happiness in our lives. So, take some time to explore the natural world around you, and let its beauty and wonder uplift and rejuvenate your soul. Embrace the healing power of nature and make it a part of your daily routine.

However, it's important to note that not everyone has easy access to nature, and for some, it may be challenging to connect with the natural world. In such cases, bringing elements of nature into your daily life can be a helpful alternative. For example, you can:

11: THE HEALING POWER OF NATURE: CONNECTING WITH THE NATURAL WORLD

Incorporate plants into your living space: Plants not only add beauty to your home or office, but they also purify the air and can help reduce stress and anxiety.

Listen to nature sounds: There are plenty of apps and websites that offer recordings of nature sounds, from birds chirping to waves crashing. Listening to these sounds can help you relax and feel more connected to the natural world.

Use natural materials: Using natural materials in your home, such as wood or stone, can help bring the outside world in and create a more calming and peaceful environment.

Watch nature documentaries: Watching documentaries about nature can help you learn more about the natural world and appreciate its beauty and complexity.

Ultimately, connecting with nature is about finding what works best for you and incorporating it into your daily life. By doing so, you can experience the many benefits that nature has to offer and cultivate greater inner peace and well-being.

11: THE HEALING POWER OF NATURE: CONNECTING WITH THE NATURAL WORLD

It's also worth noting that nature is not a cure-all for mental health issues, and if you are struggling with anxiety, stress, or other mental health concerns, it's important to seek professional help. A mental health professional can help you develop coping strategies and provide support as you work towards finding greater peace and well-being in your life.

In conclusion, the healing power of nature is undeniable. Whether it's taking a walk in the park, camping in the wilderness, or simply incorporating elements of nature into your daily life, connecting with the natural world can help reduce stress, promote mindfulness, and bring greater inner peace and happiness into your life. So, take some time to explore the natural world around you and see how it can transform your life for the better.

12: Finding Peace in Relationships: Nurturing Healthy Connections

Human beings are social creatures, and relationships are an essential aspect of our lives. Whether it is a romantic relationship, friendship, or a family bond, relationships are an essential part of our daily existence. Healthy relationships help us feel supported, loved, and appreciated, while toxic relationships can be a source of stress, anxiety, and emotional pain. In this chapter, we will explore how to nurture healthy connections and find peace in our relationships.

Understanding Relationships

Relationships are a two-way street, and they require effort and commitment from both parties to thrive. They can be a source of joy and fulfillment, but they can also be challenging and demanding. A healthy relationship is characterized by trust, respect, open communication, and a willingness to compromise.

However, it is essential to note that relationships can come in different shapes and forms, and each relationship has its unique challenges. For example, romantic relationships require emotional intimacy, vulnerability, and commitment, while friendships require loyalty, trust, and support. Therefore, it is crucial to understand the nature of the relationship and set realistic expectations.

The Importance of Self-Love

Before we can nurture healthy relationships with others, we need to first cultivate self-love and self-acceptance. Self-love is not about being selfish or narcissistic; rather, it is about treating ourselves with kindness, compassion, and respect. When we love and accept ourselves, we are more likely to attract healthy and positive relationships.

On the other hand, if we have low self-esteem, we may attract toxic relationships that feed into our insecurities and fears. Therefore, it is crucial to practice self-care, self-compassion, and self-awareness. This includes taking care of our physical, emotional, and spiritual needs and setting healthy boundaries.

Communication is Key

Open communication is a crucial element in nurturing

healthy relationships. Communication involves both listening and speaking. When we listen actively and empathetically, we show our partners, friends, or family members that we value their opinions and feelings. On the other hand, when we speak honestly and assertively, we express our own needs and boundaries.

However, effective communication is not always easy. We all have different communication styles, and sometimes we may misunderstand each other. It is crucial to practice active listening, clarify any misunderstandings, and be willing to compromise.

Conflict Resolution

Conflict is a natural part of any relationship. However, how we handle conflict can determine whether the relationship remains healthy or becomes toxic. Avoiding conflict or suppressing our feelings can lead to resentment and emotional distancing. On the other hand, attacking, blaming, or criticizing the other person can escalate the conflict and damage the relationship.

Therefore, it is essential to learn how to resolve conflicts in a healthy and constructive manner. This includes identifying the root cause of the conflict, expressing our feelings and needs, and being willing to listen to the other person's perspective. We can also seek the help of a mediator or a therapist if the conflict seems unresolvable.

Building Trust

Trust is a fundamental element in any healthy relationship. When we trust someone, we feel safe, secure, and comfortable. However, trust takes time and effort to build. It requires honesty, integrity, and consistency. We can build trust by keeping our promises, being reliable, and respecting the other person's boundaries.

On the other hand, if trust is broken, it can be challenging to rebuild. This requires sincere apologies, making amends, and demonstrating a commitment to change. It may also require seeking professional help to address underlying issues that may have contributed to the breach of trust.

Forgiveness and Letting Go

Forgiveness and letting go are essential aspects of nurturing healthy relationships. Holding onto grudges or resentments can create a toxic environment and damage the relationship. Forgiveness is not about excusing or condoning harmful behavior; rather, it is about letting go of anger and resentment and choosing to move forward. When we forgive someone, we release ourselves from the burden of negative emotions and create space for healing and growth.

Letting go also means accepting that not all relationships are meant to last. Sometimes, despite our best efforts, a relationship may become toxic or incompatible. In such cases, it is crucial to acknowledge the situation and make the difficult decision to end the relationship.

Practicing Gratitude

Gratitude is a powerful tool that can transform our relationships and our lives. When we focus on what we appreciate and value in our relationships, we create a positive and nurturing environment. Gratitude helps us to recognize the efforts and contributions of others, and it encourages us to reciprocate with kindness and generosity.

We can practice gratitude by expressing appreciation and

gratitude towards our loved ones regularly. This can be as simple as saying "thank you" or offering a compliment. We can also keep a gratitude journal or practice meditation to cultivate a sense of gratitude and mindfulness.

Cultivating Empathy and Compassion

Empathy and compassion are essential qualities that enable us to connect deeply with others and understand their perspectives and experiences. When we practice empathy and compassion, we create a safe and supportive space for our loved ones to express themselves and feel heard and understood.

We can cultivate empathy and compassion by putting ourselves in the other person's shoes and imagining how they may be feeling. We can also practice active listening and validating their feelings and experiences. Finally, we can practice self-compassion, which allows us to extend compassion and kindness towards ourselves and others.

Honoring Boundaries

Boundaries are essential in any healthy relationship. They

help us to define and protect our physical, emotional, and spiritual needs and create a sense of safety and security. Honoring boundaries means respecting the other person's limits and being willing to communicate and negotiate our own boundaries.

Setting and enforcing boundaries can be challenging, especially if we fear rejection or conflict. However, it is crucial to recognize that boundaries are necessary for our well-being and the well-being of our relationships. We can communicate our boundaries assertively and respectfully, and we can seek support from a therapist or coach if needed.

Embracing Imperfection

Finally, it is essential to embrace imperfection in our relationships. No relationship is perfect, and there will be times when we make mistakes, hurt each other, or experience conflict. However, when we accept and embrace imperfection, we create a sense of freedom and authenticity.

We can embrace imperfection by recognizing that we are all human and prone to mistakes and flaws. We can practice self-compassion and forgiveness when we make mistakes, and we can offer the same to our loved ones. Finally, we can celebrate our strengths and successes and learn from our challenges and failures.

Conclusion

Nurturing healthy relationships is a lifelong journey that requires commitment, effort, and self-awareness. By cultivating self-love, practicing effective communication, resolving conflicts, building trust, forgiving and letting go, practicing gratitude, cultivating empathy and compassion, honoring boundaries, and embracing imperfection, we can create fulfilling and joyful connections with our loved ones. Ultimately, healthy relationships are a source of inner peace and happiness and enable us to live a fulfilling and purposeful existence.

13: The Role of Forgiveness in Achieving Inner Peace

Forgiveness is a powerful tool that can help individuals achieve inner peace. It is an act of letting go of anger, resentment, and bitterness towards someone who has wronged us. When we forgive, we release ourselves from the emotional burden of holding onto negative emotions, which can lead to anxiety, stress, and negativity. Forgiveness is not always easy, but it is an essential step towards achieving inner peace.

In this chapter, we will explore the role of forgiveness in achieving inner peace. We will discuss what forgiveness means, why it is essential, and how to forgive others and yourself. We will also look at the benefits of forgiveness and how it can positively impact our lives.

What is Forgiveness?

Forgiveness is the act of letting go of negative emotions towards someone who has wronged us. It involves releasing resentment, bitterness, anger, and other negative emotions that we may have towards that person. Forgiveness does not mean that we forget or condone the wrong that was done to us. It means that we no longer allow the negative emotions associated with the wrong to control our lives.

Forgiveness is not always easy. It can be challenging to let go of the hurt and pain that we have experienced. However, forgiveness is essential if we want to achieve inner peace. When we forgive, we release ourselves from the emotional burden that we have been carrying, which can lead to feelings of relief, freedom, and peace.

Why is Forgiveness Essential?

Forgiveness is essential for several reasons. First, forgiveness allows us to let go of negative emotions that can hold us back from experiencing joy and happiness. When we hold onto anger, resentment, and bitterness, we create negative energy that can impact our physical, emotional, and mental well-being.

Second, forgiveness can improve our relationships with others. When we hold onto negative emotions towards someone, it can create a barrier between us and that person. Forgiveness allows us to break down that barrier and rebuild trust and connection with others.

13: THE ROLE OF FORGIVENESS IN ACHIEVING INNER PEACE

Finally, forgiveness is essential for our spiritual growth. Forgiveness is a fundamental principle in many spiritual traditions, including Christianity, Buddhism, and Islam. Forgiveness is seen as an act of compassion and love, and it can help us grow spiritually and deepen our connection with a higher power.

How to Forgive Others and Yourself

Forgiveness is not always easy, but it is possible. Here are some steps that you can take to forgive others and yourself:

Acknowledge the hurt and pain that you have experienced. It is essential to acknowledge the pain that you have experienced and the emotions associated with it. Recognizing the pain can help you begin the process of letting go.

Choose to forgive. Forgiveness is a choice. You can choose to hold onto anger, resentment, and bitterness, or you can choose to let it go and forgive.

Practice empathy. Try to see things from the other person's perspective. Understanding why someone may have hurt you can help you empathize with them and begin to let go of negative emotions.

Let go of negative emotions. It is essential to release negative emotions such as anger, resentment, and bitterness. You can do this through mindfulness techniques such as meditation, deep breathing, and visualization.

Take responsibility for your actions. If you have hurt someone else, it is essential to take responsibility for your actions and apologize. Taking responsibility can help you forgive yourself and move forward.

The Benefits of Forgiveness

Forgiveness has numerous benefits. Here are some of the ways that forgiveness can positively impact our lives:

Improved mental health. Forgiveness can reduce symptoms of anxiety, depression, and stress. Letting go of negative emotions can improve our mental health and well-being.

Improved relationships. Forgiveness can improve our relationships with others. Letting go of negative emotions towards someone can help us build trust and connection with them.

13: THE ROLE OF FORGIVENESS IN ACHIEVING INNER PEACE

Increased empathy and compassion. Forgiveness can increase our ability to empathize with others and show compassion towards them.

Reduced anger and resentment. Forgiveness can help reduce feelings of anger and resentment towards someone who has wronged us.

Increased self-esteem. Forgiveness can increase our self-esteem by helping us let go of negative self-talk and self-blame.

Improved physical health. Forgiveness has been shown to have a positive impact on physical health. It can lower blood pressure, reduce pain, and boost the immune system.

Spiritual growth. Forgiveness is an essential aspect of many spiritual traditions, and it can help us grow spiritually and deepen our connection with a higher power.

In conclusion, forgiveness is an essential tool for achieving inner peace. It allows us to let go of negative emotions and move forward with our lives. Forgiveness is not always easy, but it is possible. By acknowledging our pain, choosing to

13: THE ROLE OF FORGIVENESS IN ACHIEVING INNER PEACE

forgive, practicing empathy, letting go of negative emotions, and taking responsibility for our actions, we can experience the benefits of forgiveness and achieve inner peace.

14: Cultivating Self-Compassion: Learning to Love Yourself

As human beings, we often find ourselves constantly seeking the approval and acceptance of others. We tend to be our own harshest critics and judges, always comparing ourselves to others and measuring our self-worth based on external factors. This negative self-talk and self-criticism can lead to feelings of anxiety, stress, and even depression.

However, the key to living a fulfilling and joyful existence is to cultivate self-compassion and learn to love yourself unconditionally. Self-compassion involves treating yourself with the same kindness, care, and concern that you would offer to a dear friend. It is about accepting your imperfections, embracing your strengths, and recognizing that you are worthy of love and respect just as you are.

So, how do you cultivate self-compassion? Here are some proven self-help strategies, mindfulness techniques, and spiritual practices that can help you learn to love yourself and experience the life-changing power of inner peace.

Practice Mindfulness Meditation

14: CULTIVATING SELF-COMPASSION: LEARNING TO LOVE YOURSELF

Mindfulness meditation is a powerful tool for cultivating self-compassion. It involves being present in the moment, observing your thoughts and feelings without judgment, and accepting yourself as you are. Mindfulness meditation can help you become more aware of your negative self-talk and replace it with positive, self-affirming thoughts.

To practice mindfulness meditation, find a quiet place where you can sit comfortably without distractions. Close your eyes and focus on your breath, feeling the sensation of the air moving in and out of your body. Whenever your mind wanders, gently bring it back to your breath. As you meditate, observe any thoughts or feelings that arise without judgment or attachment. Simply acknowledge them and let them go, returning your focus to your breath.

Practice Self-Compassionate Writing

Writing can be a powerful tool for cultivating self-compassion. Writing down your thoughts and feelings can help you gain insight into your negative self-talk and identify patterns of self-criticism. Self-compassionate writing involves writing down your self-critical thoughts and then reframing them in a positive, self-affirming way.

14: CULTIVATING SELF-COMPASSION: LEARNING TO LOVE YOURSELF

To practice self-compassionate writing, start by writing down any negative thoughts or feelings that come to mind. Then, for each thought, ask yourself what you would say to a dear friend who was experiencing the same thing. Write down a compassionate and supportive response, as if you were speaking to that friend. This exercise can help you learn to treat yourself with the same kindness and care that you would offer to others.

Practice Gratitude

Gratitude is a powerful practice for cultivating self-compassion. It involves focusing on the things in your life that you are grateful for, rather than dwelling on your shortcomings or failures. Gratitude can help you shift your perspective from one of lack and negativity to one of abundance and positivity.

To practice gratitude, take a few moments each day to reflect on the things in your life that you are grateful for. You can write them down in a journal or simply reflect on them in your mind. Focus on the people, experiences, and things that bring you joy and fulfillment, and express gratitude for them. This practice can help you cultivate a sense of self-worth and appreciation for all that you have in your life.

Practice Self-Care

Self-care is an essential aspect of cultivating self-compassion. It involves taking care of your physical, emotional, and spiritual well-being and treating yourself with kindness and care. Self-care can include things like eating a healthy diet, getting enough sleep, exercising regularly, spending time in nature, practicing relaxation techniques, and engaging in activities that bring you joy.

To practice self-care, start by identifying the things that make you feel good and prioritize them in your life. Make time for activities that nourish your body, mind, and spirit, and don't feel guilty about taking time for yourself. Remember that you are worthy of care and attention, and that taking care of yourself is essential for your overall well-being.

Practice Affirmations

Affirmations are positive statements that you repeat to yourself to help shift your mindset and overcome negative self-talk. Affirmations can help you cultivate self-compassion by focusing your attention on your strengths and positive qualities, rather than your shortcomings or failures.

To practice affirmations, choose a few positive statements that resonate with you and repeat them to yourself throughout the day. You can write them down and place them in a visible location, or simply repeat them in your mind. Some examples of affirmations include "I am worthy of love and respect," "I am capable and strong," and "I am deserving of happiness and joy."

Practice Forgiveness

Forgiveness is an essential aspect of cultivating self-compassion. It involves letting go of grudges and resentments and treating yourself with kindness and understanding, even when you make mistakes. Forgiveness can help you release negative emotions and move forward with compassion and grace.

To practice forgiveness, start by forgiving yourself for any mistakes or shortcomings. Remember that making mistakes is a natural part of the human experience, and that you are not defined by your failures. Offer yourself the same forgiveness and understanding that you would offer to a dear friend, and let go of any self-judgment or self-criticism.

In conclusion, cultivating self-compassion is an essential aspect of living a fulfilling and joyful existence. By practicing mindfulness meditation, self-compassionate writing, gratitude, self-care, affirmations, and forgiveness, you can learn to treat yourself with kindness, care, and understanding. Remember that self-compassion is not a one-time event, but a lifelong practice. With dedication and commitment, you can experience the life-changing power of inner peace and embrace a fulfilling and joyful existence.

15: Overcoming Fear and Anxiety through Spiritual Practice

Fear and anxiety are emotions that most people experience at some point in their lives. These emotions can be triggered by various factors, including traumatic experiences, phobias, and stressful situations. Although it is natural to feel anxious or fearful in certain situations, when these emotions become overwhelming and persistent, they can lead to significant emotional and physical distress.

In this chapter, we will explore how spiritual practice can help individuals overcome fear and anxiety. We will begin by discussing the root causes of fear and anxiety and how spiritual practice can address these causes. We will then discuss specific spiritual practices that can be used to promote inner peace and reduce anxiety.

The Root Causes of Fear and Anxiety

Fear and anxiety are often caused by our thoughts and beliefs about ourselves and the world around us. For example, we may feel anxious about speaking in public because we believe that we will be judged or criticized by others. Similarly, we may experience fear when we encounter a spider because we believe that it poses a threat to our safety.

These thoughts and beliefs are often based on our past experiences and the messages we have received from society and our culture. For example, if we grew up in a family that emphasized the importance of success and achievement, we may develop a fear of failure. Similarly, if we live in a society that values youth and beauty, we may feel anxious about aging.

Spiritual Practice and Overcoming Fear and Anxiety

Spiritual practice can help individuals overcome fear and anxiety by addressing the root causes of these emotions. Spiritual practice involves cultivating a connection with something greater than ourselves, such as a higher power, the universe, or our own inner wisdom. This connection can provide us with a sense of purpose, meaning, and guidance that can help us navigate difficult emotions and experiences.

One of the most effective spiritual practices for overcoming fear and anxiety is mindfulness meditation. Mindfulness meditation involves focusing our attention on the present moment, without judgment or distraction. This practice can help us become more aware of our thoughts and beliefs about ourselves and the world around us, and can help us develop a more compassionate and non-judgmental relationship with ourselves.

Another spiritual practice that can be effective in overcoming fear and anxiety is prayer. Prayer involves communicating with a higher power or divine force, and can provide us with a sense of comfort, support, and guidance. Prayer can also help us feel more connected to something greater than ourselves, which can help us feel less alone and isolated in our struggles.

In addition to mindfulness meditation and prayer, there are many other spiritual practices that can be helpful in overcoming fear and anxiety. These include:

Yoga: Yoga is a spiritual practice that involves physical postures, breath control, and meditation. It can help us develop greater physical and emotional awareness, reduce stress and anxiety, and promote inner peace.

Gratitude: Gratitude involves cultivating a sense of appreciation and thankfulness for the people, experiences, and things in our lives. This practice can help us shift our focus from what we lack to what we have, and can help us feel more content and fulfilled.

Forgiveness: Forgiveness involves letting go of anger, resentment, and bitterness towards ourselves and others. This practice can help us release negative emotions that may be contributing to our anxiety and fear, and can help us develop greater compassion and empathy.

Self-compassion: Self-compassion involves treating ourselves with kindness, understanding, and acceptance, especially when we are struggling with difficult emotions or experiences. This practice can help us develop greater resilience and emotional strength, and can help us feel more connected to ourselves and others.

Service: Service involves helping others and contributing to the greater good. This practice can help us feel more connected to something greater than ourselves, and can help us develop a sense of purpose and meaning in our lives.

Integrating Spiritual Practices into Daily Life

15: OVERCOMING FEAR AND ANXIETY THROUGH SPIRITUAL PRACTICE

While spiritual practices can be powerful tools for overcoming fear and anxiety, it can be challenging to integrate these practices into our daily lives. Here are some tips for making spiritual practices a regular part of your routine:

Start small: Begin by incorporating a small spiritual practice into your daily routine, such as a five-minute mindfulness meditation or a quick prayer of gratitude before meals. As you become more comfortable with these practices, you can gradually increase the amount of time you spend on them.

Set aside dedicated time: Choose a specific time of day to engage in your spiritual practice, such as first thing in the morning or before bed. By making your spiritual practice a regular part of your routine, you can create a sense of ritual and structure around your practice.

Find a community: Seek out a community of like-minded individuals who share your spiritual beliefs and practices. This can provide you with support, encouragement, and inspiration as you work to overcome fear and anxiety.

Be patient and persistent: Remember that overcoming fear and anxiety is a journey, and it may take time and practice to see significant results. Be patient and persistent, and celebrate small victories along the way.

In Conclusion

Fear and anxiety can be debilitating emotions that can interfere with our ability to live a fulfilling and joyful life. However, by engaging in spiritual practices, we can develop the inner strength, resilience, and peace that can help us overcome these emotions and live our best lives. Whether it is through mindfulness meditation, prayer, yoga, gratitude, forgiveness, self-compassion, or service, there are many spiritual practices that can help us cultivate a sense of inner peace and joy that can transform our lives.

16: Developing Resilience: Building Strength and Coping Skills

Life can be tough. It's filled with unexpected twists and turns, setbacks and disappointments. Challenges come in all shapes and sizes, and we are often tested in ways that we never anticipated. Whether it's the loss of a loved one, a health crisis, a job loss, or any other difficulty, we all face adversity at some point in our lives. The question is, how do we respond to these challenges? Do we crumble under the weight of them, or do we rise up and face them head-on?

The answer lies in developing resilience. Resilience is the ability to bounce back from adversity, to persevere in the face of difficulty, and to come out stronger on the other side. Resilience is not something that we are born with; rather, it is a skill that can be developed and honed over time. In this chapter, we will explore the concept of resilience and provide you with practical strategies to help you build resilience in your own life.

The Importance of Resilience

Resilience is essential for our mental health and well-being. Without resilience, we can become overwhelmed by stress, anxiety, and negativity. We may feel helpless and powerless in the face of challenges, and this can lead to feelings of despair and hopelessness. Resilience allows us to maintain a positive outlook in the face of adversity, to stay focused on our goals, and to persevere even when the going gets tough.

Resilience is also important for our physical health. Chronic stress and anxiety can take a toll on our bodies, leading to a host of health problems, including heart disease, high blood pressure, and obesity. Resilience helps us to manage stress and to avoid these negative health outcomes.

Finally, resilience is important for our relationships. When we are resilient, we are better able to connect with others and to form strong, healthy relationships. We are more empathetic and compassionate, and we are better equipped to handle conflict and resolve differences.

Building Resilience

So, how do we build resilience? There are several strategies that can help us develop this essential skill.

Cultivate a positive mindset

16: DEVELOPING RESILIENCE: BUILDING STRENGTH AND COPING SKILLS

One of the most important aspects of resilience is having a positive mindset. When we approach challenges with a positive attitude, we are better able to find solutions and to bounce back from setbacks. To cultivate a positive mindset, try focusing on your strengths and accomplishments, practicing gratitude, and reframing negative thoughts into positive ones.

Develop a support system

Having a support system is essential for resilience. We all need people who we can turn to for emotional support and encouragement. This might include family members, friends, or a therapist. Make an effort to build and nurture these relationships, and be willing to ask for help when you need it.

Take care of yourself

Self-care is crucial for resilience. This means taking care of your physical, emotional, and spiritual health. Get enough sleep, eat a healthy diet, exercise regularly, and practice stress-reducing activities like meditation or yoga. Take time to do things that bring you joy and fulfillment, and make self-care a priority in your daily life.

Set goals

Setting goals can help us stay focused and motivated, even in the face of challenges. Make a list of short-term and long-term goals, and create a plan for achieving them. Celebrate your successes along the way, and use setbacks as opportunities to learn and grow.

Practice mindfulness

Mindfulness is a powerful tool for building resilience. When we practice mindfulness, we learn to be present in the moment and to observe our thoughts and emotions without judgment. This can help us to manage stress and anxiety, and to develop a more positive outlook on life.

Practice self-compassion

Finally, it's important to practice self-compassion when building resilience. Self-compassion means treating yourself with kindness and understanding, especially when you are struggling or facing challenges. This includes being patient with yourself, recognizing that setbacks are a natural part of the process, and avoiding self-criticism.

Developing resilience takes time and effort, but the benefits are well worth it. With resilience, you can face life's challenges with confidence and strength, and come out the other side with a greater sense of self-awareness and personal growth.

Overcoming Obstacles

Even with the best strategies for building resilience, obstacles will inevitably arise. When this happens, it's important to stay focused and to keep moving forward. Here are some additional tips for overcoming obstacles:

Stay flexible

Flexibility is key when it comes to resilience. Be open to new ideas and approaches, and be willing to adjust your goals and plans as needed.

Practice problem-solving

When faced with obstacles, try to approach the problem in a systematic way. Break the problem down into smaller, more manageable pieces, and brainstorm possible solutions. Consider the pros and cons of each option, and choose the best course of action.

Embrace the process

Remember that building resilience is a process, and setbacks are a natural part of that process. Be patient with yourself, and use setbacks as opportunities to learn and grow.

Stay connected

Stay connected with your support system, and reach out to others for help and encouragement when you need it. Remember that you are not alone, and that others have faced similar challenges and overcome them.

Practice self-care

Self-care is especially important when facing obstacles. Make sure to take care of your physical, emotional, and spiritual health, and practice stress-reducing activities like meditation or yoga.

16: DEVELOPING RESILIENCE: BUILDING STRENGTH AND COPING SKILLS

Conclusion

In conclusion, developing resilience is essential for our mental, physical, and emotional well-being. With resilience, we are better able to face life's challenges, bounce back from setbacks, and come out the other side stronger and more self-aware. By cultivating a positive mindset, building a support system, practicing self-care, setting goals, practicing mindfulness, and practicing self-compassion, we can develop the skills we need to be more resilient. And when obstacles arise, staying flexible, practicing problem-solving, embracing the process, staying connected, and practicing self-care can help us to overcome them. Remember, resilience is a skill that can be developed over time, and the more we practice it, the stronger and more resilient we will become.

17: Finding Meaning and Purpose: Connecting with Your Inner Self

Introduction:

The search for meaning and purpose is an essential part of the human experience. We all want to feel like we have a reason for being, that our lives matter, and that we are making a difference in the world. However, the quest for meaning and purpose can be challenging, especially in today's fast-paced and often chaotic world. Many people feel lost, disconnected, and unfulfilled, and they don't know where to turn.

Fortunately, finding meaning and purpose is possible. In this chapter, we will explore the importance of connecting with your inner self, and how this can help you discover your life's purpose. We will also explore self-help strategies, mindfulness techniques, and spiritual practices that can assist you in your journey towards inner peace, fulfillment, and joy.

The Importance of Connecting with Your Inner Self:

Connecting with your inner self is vital to discovering meaning and purpose. When you are in touch with your inner self, you are more aware of your thoughts, feelings, and beliefs. You understand yourself on a deeper level, and you have a clearer understanding of what you want and need in life.

Unfortunately, many people are out of touch with their inner selves. They are so busy with the demands of daily life that they don't take the time to reflect on their thoughts and feelings. As a result, they feel disconnected, unfulfilled, and unsure of what they want out of life.

To connect with your inner self, you need to make time for self-reflection. This means taking a break from the distractions of daily life and spending time alone with your thoughts. You can do this through meditation, journaling, or simply taking a quiet walk in nature.

Self-Help Strategies:

Self-help strategies can also be helpful in discovering meaning and purpose. These are practical techniques that you can use to improve your mental health and wellbeing, and they can help you gain a better understanding of yourself.

17: FINDING MEANING AND PURPOSE: CONNECTING WITH YOUR INNER SELF

One self-help strategy that can be particularly useful is cognitive-behavioral therapy (CBT). CBT is a type of therapy that helps you identify negative thought patterns and replace them with more positive ones. By changing the way you think, you can improve your mental health and well-being, and develop a clearer sense of purpose in life.

Another self-help strategy that can be helpful is goal setting. Setting goals can help you focus your energy and efforts on what matters most to you. When you have a clear goal in mind, you are more likely to take action towards achieving it, which can give you a sense of purpose and fulfillment.

Mindfulness Techniques:

Mindfulness techniques can also be helpful in discovering meaning and purpose. Mindfulness is the practice of being present in the moment, without judgment or distraction. By being mindful, you can tune into your thoughts and feelings, and gain a deeper understanding of yourself.

One mindfulness technique that can be particularly helpful is mindful breathing. This involves taking deep breaths and focusing on your breath as it moves in and out of your body.

17: FINDING MEANING AND PURPOSE: CONNECTING WITH YOUR INNER SELF

By focusing on your breath, you can calm your mind and reduce stress and anxiety.

Another mindfulness technique that can be helpful is body scanning. This involves paying attention to different parts of your body and noticing any sensations or feelings that arise. By doing a body scan, you can become more aware of any physical tension or discomfort, and learn to release it through relaxation techniques.

Spiritual Practices:

Spiritual practices can also be helpful in discovering meaning and purpose. These practices can help you connect with something greater than yourself, and give you a sense of purpose and direction in life.

One spiritual practice that can be helpful is meditation. Meditation is a practice of quieting the mind and connecting with your inner self. By meditating, you can gain clarity and insight into your thoughts and feelings, and develop a deeper sense of purpose and connection with the world around you.

Another spiritual practice that can be helpful is yoga. Yoga is a physical and spiritual practice that involves poses, breathing techniques, and meditation. By practicing yoga, you can improve your physical health and wellbeing, reduce stress and anxiety, and develop a deeper connection with your inner self and the world around you.

Other spiritual practices that can be helpful include prayer, mindfulness, and gratitude. Prayer is a way of connecting with a higher power, and can give you a sense of purpose and direction in life. Mindfulness is the practice of being present in the moment, and can help you become more aware of your thoughts and feelings. Gratitude is the practice of being thankful for the blessings in your life, and can help you develop a positive and optimistic outlook.

Conclusion:

Finding meaning and purpose is an essential part of the human experience. By connecting with your inner self, and using self-help strategies, mindfulness techniques, and spiritual practices, you can discover your life's purpose and live a fulfilling and joyful existence. Remember to take the time to reflect on your thoughts and feelings, set clear goals, and practice self-care and self-compassion. By doing so, you can develop a deeper understanding of yourself, and find meaning and purpose in your life.

18: Letting Go of Control: Surrendering to the Flow of Life

As human beings, we have a natural tendency to want to control every aspect of our lives. We crave certainty and stability, and we fear the unknown. We want to know what will happen in the future, and we want to be prepared for every possible outcome. We try to control our environment, our relationships, our emotions, and even our thoughts. We believe that by controlling everything, we will be able to avoid pain, disappointment, and failure.

However, this need for control often backfires, causing us more stress, anxiety, and frustration. We become so focused on trying to control everything that we forget to live in the present moment. We miss out on the joy and beauty of life because we are so preoccupied with trying to prevent the worst from happening.

The truth is, we cannot control everything. Life is unpredictable and constantly changing. No matter how much we plan and prepare, unexpected events can happen at any time. We may lose our job, get sick, or experience a relationship breakdown. We cannot control the actions of others or the forces of nature. We cannot control the past or the future.

The only thing we can control is our response to these events. We can choose to react with fear, anger, and resistance, or we can choose to respond with acceptance, compassion, and openness. We can learn to let go of our need for control and surrender to the flow of life.

Letting go of control does not mean giving up on our goals and dreams. It does not mean that we should stop working hard or stop making plans for the future. It simply means that we should let go of our attachment to the outcome. We should focus on the present moment and trust that everything will unfold as it should.

Surrendering to the flow of life requires a shift in mindset. We must learn to embrace uncertainty and trust in the universe. We must learn to let go of our expectations and surrender to the present moment. We must learn to be patient and allow things to unfold naturally.

One way to cultivate this mindset is through mindfulness practices. Mindfulness teaches us to be fully present in the moment and to observe our thoughts and emotions without judgment. It helps us to let go of our attachment to the past and the future and to focus on the present moment.

Another way to let go of control is through spiritual practices. Many spiritual traditions teach the importance of surrender and trust in a higher power. By letting go of our ego and surrendering to a higher power, we can experience a sense of peace and serenity.

Ultimately, letting go of control is about surrendering to the mystery of life. It is about trusting that everything happens for a reason and that everything will work out in the end. It is about embracing the uncertainty of life and finding joy and beauty in the present moment.

In conclusion, letting go of control is a powerful way to overcome anxiety, stress, and negativity and to embrace a fulfilling and joyful existence. By surrendering to the flow of life and letting go of our attachment to the outcome, we can experience a sense of peace and freedom. We can learn to trust in ourselves and in the universe and live our lives with greater ease and grace.

19: The Power of Positive Affirmations: Changing Your Inner Dialogue

Introduction:

Have you ever caught yourself repeating negative self-talk or destructive thought patterns? Perhaps you tell yourself that you're not good enough, smart enough, or deserving of happiness. Or maybe you focus on all the things that could go wrong in a situation, rather than embracing the possibilities for success and growth.

Negative self-talk can be incredibly damaging to your mental and emotional health, leading to anxiety, depression, and a sense of hopelessness. But what if there was a way to change your inner dialogue, to shift your focus from negative to positive, and to cultivate a deep sense of inner peace and happiness?

In this chapter, we'll explore the power of positive affirmations as a tool for transforming your mindset and creating a more fulfilling and joyful existence. We'll delve into what affirmations are, how they work, and how you can start incorporating them into your daily routine.

19: THE POWER OF POSITIVE AFFIRMATIONS: CHANGING YOUR INNER DIALOGUE

What are Affirmations?

At its core, an affirmation is simply a statement of belief or intention. It's a positive statement that you repeat to yourself, often with the intention of changing your thought patterns or beliefs about yourself and the world around you.

Affirmations can be simple or complex, depending on your needs and preferences. Some people prefer short, simple affirmations that they can repeat easily throughout the day, while others enjoy longer, more detailed statements that they can reflect on and internalize over time.

Examples of affirmations might include:

– I am worthy of love and respect

– I trust that everything will work out for my highest good

– I am capable of achieving my goals and dreams

– I am strong, confident, and resilient

– I am filled with joy and gratitude for all that I have

How do Affirmations Work?

19: THE POWER OF POSITIVE AFFIRMATIONS: CHANGING YOUR INNER DIALOGUE

At first glance, affirmations might seem like nothing more than positive statements that you repeat to yourself. But the truth is, affirmations can have a powerful impact on your mindset and behavior.

When you repeat an affirmation to yourself, you're essentially reprogramming your subconscious mind. Your subconscious is the part of your mind that's responsible for your beliefs, habits, and automatic responses to situations.

If your subconscious is filled with negative beliefs and thought patterns, it can be difficult to change your behavior or outlook on life. But by repeating positive affirmations, you can start to shift those negative beliefs and replace them with more empowering and supportive ones.

Over time, affirmations can help you to:

– Boost your self-confidence and self-esteem

– Overcome negative thought patterns and self-talk

– Reduce stress and anxiety

– Cultivate a sense of inner peace and calm

19: THE POWER OF POSITIVE AFFIRMATIONS: CHANGING YOUR INNER DIALOGUE

– Attract more positivity and abundance into your life

– Improve your relationships and communication skills

How to Use Affirmations:

If you're new to affirmations, it can be helpful to start with just one or two that resonate with you. Choose affirmations that reflect your goals, desires, and areas of self-improvement.

Here are some tips for using affirmations effectively:

Repeat your affirmations regularly: To see the most benefit from affirmations, it's important to repeat them consistently. Some people like to set aside time each day to repeat their affirmations, while others prefer to integrate them into their daily routine (e.g., repeating affirmations while brushing your teeth or driving to work).

Use present tense: When crafting your affirmations, use present tense language to create a sense of immediacy and impact. For example, instead of saying "I will be happy," say "I am happy."

Make them personal: Affirmations are most effective when they're tailored to your individual needs and beliefs. Use language that feels authentic and empowering to you, rather than simply repeating generic affirmations that don't resonate with your experience.

Believe in them: To get the most out of your affirmations, it's important to believe in them. This can be a bit challenging at first, especially if you've spent years telling yourself negative messages. However, the more you repeat your affirmations, the more they'll become a natural part of your thought process.

Visualize the outcome: When repeating your affirmations, try to imagine the outcome you want to achieve. For example, if your affirmation is "I am confident and capable," picture yourself confidently completing a task or achieving a goal. This visualization can help reinforce your affirmation and make it more real for you.

Mix it up: To keep your affirmations fresh and interesting, mix up your statements from time to time. You might add new affirmations as you achieve certain goals or shift your focus to new areas of improvement.

19: THE POWER OF POSITIVE AFFIRMATIONS: CHANGING YOUR INNER DIALOGUE

Examples of Affirmations:

Here are some examples of affirmations that you might find helpful:

– I am worthy of love and respect, just as I am.

– I trust that the universe is conspiring in my favor, and everything will work out for my highest good.

– I am confident and capable of achieving my goals and dreams.

– I am grateful for all that I have and all that I am.

– I am strong, resilient, and capable of overcoming any challenge.

– I embrace my uniqueness and honor my true self.

– I let go of negative self-talk and embrace positivity and self-love.

– I am deserving of abundance and prosperity in all areas of my life.

19: THE POWER OF POSITIVE AFFIRMATIONS: CHANGING YOUR INNER DIALOGUE

– I am open to new experiences and opportunities for growth and learning.

– I choose to live in the present moment and appreciate the beauty around me.

Conclusion:

Positive affirmations can be a powerful tool for transforming your mindset and creating a more fulfilling and joyful existence. By repeating affirmations regularly, you can reprogram your subconscious mind and replace negative beliefs and thought patterns with more empowering and supportive ones.

Remember, the key to effective affirmations is repetition, authenticity, and belief. Choose affirmations that resonate with your individual needs and beliefs, and repeat them consistently to see the most benefit.

With time and practice, you can change your inner dialogue and cultivate a deep sense of inner peace and happiness.

20: Navigating Difficult Emotions: Facing Your Fears

Introduction

Emotions are a part of our daily lives. They help us connect with the world around us and make us human. However, not all emotions are easy to handle. There are times when we feel overwhelmed and unable to cope with our emotions. These emotions can lead to anxiety, stress, and negativity, which can significantly impact our well-being. In this chapter, we will explore how to navigate difficult emotions and face our fears.

Understanding Difficult Emotions

Difficult emotions are those that are uncomfortable, distressing, and challenging to manage. Examples include anger, fear, sadness, shame, guilt, and jealousy. These emotions can be triggered by various factors, such as stress, traumatic experiences, relationship issues, health problems, or negative self-talk.

Many of us tend to avoid these emotions or suppress them, thinking that it's the best way to deal with them. However, avoiding these emotions can lead to more significant problems in the long run. Bottling up emotions can lead to physical and mental health issues, relationship problems, and a general feeling of dissatisfaction and unhappiness.

The key to navigating difficult emotions is to acknowledge them and accept them for what they are. It's okay to feel angry, sad, or scared. These emotions are a part of our human experience. By acknowledging these emotions, we can take the first step towards managing them effectively.

Facing Your Fears

Fear is a powerful emotion that can hold us back from achieving our goals and living a fulfilling life. Whether it's fear of failure, fear of rejection, or fear of the unknown, fear can prevent us from taking risks and pursuing our dreams.

The first step in facing your fears is to identify them. Ask yourself, "What am I afraid of?" Once you've identified your fears, it's essential to examine them and determine if they're rational or irrational.

For example, if you're afraid of public speaking, ask yourself, "What's the worst that can happen?" The worst-case scenario might be that you forget your lines, stumble over your words, or receive negative feedback. While these outcomes might be uncomfortable, they're not life-threatening or irreversible.

Once you've identified your fears and examined them, it's time to take action. One way to face your fears is to expose yourself to them gradually. For example, if you're afraid of heights, start by standing on a low platform or a step ladder. Then, gradually work your way up to higher heights.

Another way to face your fears is to reframe your thinking. Instead of focusing on the negative outcomes, focus on the positive ones. For example, if you're afraid of taking risks, focus on the potential rewards that come with taking those risks.

Managing Difficult Emotions

Managing difficult emotions is an essential part of navigating them effectively. Here are some proven strategies for managing difficult emotions:

20: NAVIGATING DIFFICULT EMOTIONS: FACING YOUR FEARS

Mindfulness: Mindfulness involves paying attention to the present moment without judgment. Mindfulness can help you become more aware of your thoughts and emotions and help you manage them more effectively.

Self-compassion: Self-compassion involves treating yourself with kindness, care, and understanding. When you're experiencing difficult emotions, it's essential to be kind to yourself and offer yourself comfort and support.

Gratitude: Practicing gratitude can help you shift your focus from negative emotions to positive ones. Take time each day to reflect on the things you're grateful for.

Exercise: Exercise can help you manage stress and anxiety by releasing endorphins, which are natural mood-boosters.

Talk to someone: Talking to someone you trust can help you process your emotions and gain perspective on your situation.

Conclusion

Navigating difficult emotions is a challenging but necessary part of life. By acknowledging your emotions, facing your fears, and managing them effectively, you can live a more fulfilling and joyful existence.

Remember that it's okay to feel difficult emotions. They're a natural part of the human experience, and everyone goes through them at some point in their lives. The key is to not let them consume you and to take steps to manage them effectively.

Practicing mindfulness, self-compassion, gratitude, exercise, and talking to someone can all be helpful strategies in managing difficult emotions. However, what works for one person may not work for another, so it's essential to find what works best for you.

Finally, it's important to remember that navigating difficult emotions is not a one-time event. It's an ongoing process that requires patience, self-awareness, and perseverance. With practice and commitment, you can develop the skills to navigate difficult emotions and live a more peaceful and fulfilling life.

21: Coping with Grief and Loss: Finding Comfort in Difficult Times

Grief and loss are universal experiences that everyone will face at some point in their lives. Whether it is the loss of a loved one, a job, a relationship, or even a pet, the pain can be overwhelming and often feels insurmountable. It is natural to feel a range of emotions during the grieving process, including sadness, anger, guilt, and even numbness. However, it is important to remember that it is possible to find comfort and peace even in the midst of the most difficult times.

The first step in coping with grief and loss is to allow yourself to feel your emotions. Many people try to suppress their feelings or push them aside, but this only prolongs the grieving process. It is essential to acknowledge and accept your emotions, even if they are painful. Cry if you need to, talk to a trusted friend or therapist, or journal your thoughts and feelings. Remember that it is okay to feel sad, angry, or confused.

The next step is to take care of yourself physically and emotionally. Grief can take a toll on your body, so it is important to prioritize your physical health. Get enough sleep, eat a healthy diet, exercise regularly, and avoid unhealthy coping mechanisms such as drugs or alcohol. Additionally, take time to nurture yourself emotionally. Do things that bring you joy and comfort, such as reading a favorite book, listening to music, or spending time in nature. Practice self-compassion and be gentle with yourself during this difficult time.

One of the most powerful ways to cope with grief and loss is through mindfulness and meditation. Mindfulness involves paying attention to the present moment without judgment. When we are grieving, our minds often race with thoughts and emotions. Mindfulness can help us slow down and be more present in the moment. Start by simply observing your breath or your surroundings without trying to change anything. If your mind wanders, gently bring it back to the present moment. You can also try meditation, which involves focusing your attention on a particular object, such as a candle flame or a mantra. Meditation can help calm your mind and reduce stress and anxiety.

21: COPING WITH GRIEF AND LOSS: FINDING COMFORT IN DIFFICULT TIMES

Another way to find comfort in difficult times is through spirituality and faith. For many people, spirituality provides a sense of meaning and purpose, which can be especially helpful during times of grief and loss. Whether you find solace in a particular religion or simply in your own personal beliefs, connecting with your spirituality can help you find peace and comfort. Consider attending a religious service, reading spiritual texts, or practicing meditation or prayer.

It is also important to seek support from others. Many people try to isolate themselves during times of grief, but this only exacerbates feelings of loneliness and sadness. Reach out to friends or family members who can provide a listening ear or a shoulder to cry on. Consider joining a support group for people who are also experiencing grief and loss. Talking to others who have gone through similar experiences can be incredibly comforting and validating.

Finally, remember that healing takes time. Grief and loss are not something that can be "fixed" overnight. It is a process that requires patience, self-compassion, and perseverance. Be kind to yourself and allow yourself to grieve in your own way and at your own pace. With time, you will find that the pain lessens and that you are able to move forward with a renewed sense of purpose and inner peace.

In conclusion, coping with grief and loss is a challenging and deeply personal journey. However, by allowing yourself to feel your emotions, taking care of your physical and emotional health, practicing mindfulness and meditation, connecting with your spirituality, seeking support from others, and being patient with yourself, you can find comfort and peace even in the midst of the most difficult times. Remember that healing is possible and that you are not alone.

22: The Importance of Self-Care: Nurturing Your Mind, Body, and Soul

Introduction

We live in a fast-paced world that often leaves us feeling stressed, anxious, and overwhelmed. We have so many responsibilities, obligations, and commitments that we forget to take care of ourselves. However, neglecting our self-care can lead to physical, emotional, and mental exhaustion, which can have a detrimental effect on our well-being. In this chapter, we will discuss the importance of self-care and how it can help us nurture our mind, body, and soul.

What is Self-Care?

Self-care is the intentional and deliberate act of taking care of oneself. It involves engaging in activities that promote physical, emotional, and mental health. Self-care is not a selfish act, as some people may think. Instead, it is an essential aspect of our overall well-being. Self-care can take many forms, including getting enough sleep, eating nutritious food, exercising regularly, engaging in hobbies and interests, and practicing mindfulness and relaxation techniques.

The Importance of Self-Care

Self-care is crucial for our physical, emotional, and mental health. When we neglect self-care, we can experience burnout, stress, anxiety, depression, and other health problems. Taking care of ourselves helps us stay energized, focused, and resilient. It enables us to handle the challenges and demands of life with more ease and grace.

Physical Health

Taking care of our physical health is essential for our overall well-being. When we engage in regular physical activity, eat a nutritious diet, and get enough rest, we can maintain a healthy weight, reduce the risk of chronic diseases, and improve our cardiovascular health. Exercise releases endorphins, which are natural mood-boosters that can help reduce stress and anxiety. Eating a healthy diet can also improve our mood and energy levels, and getting enough sleep can enhance our cognitive function and productivity.

Emotional Health

22: THE IMPORTANCE OF SELF-CARE: NURTURING YOUR MIND, BODY, AND SOUL

Our emotional health is just as important as our physical health. When we take care of our emotional well-being, we can reduce the risk of developing anxiety, depression, and other mental health disorders. Engaging in activities that bring us joy, such as hobbies and interests, can improve our emotional well-being. Spending time with loved ones, practicing gratitude, and cultivating positive relationships can also enhance our emotional health.

Mental Health

Mental health is essential for our overall well-being. When we take care of our mental health, we can reduce the risk of developing mental health disorders such as anxiety, depression, and bipolar disorder. Practicing mindfulness, meditation, and relaxation techniques can help reduce stress and anxiety, and promote a sense of calm and relaxation. Engaging in activities that promote creativity, such as writing or painting, can also improve our mental health.

Self-Care Strategies

There are many self-care strategies that we can use to nurture our mind, body, and soul. Here are some examples:

Exercise regularly: Engaging in regular physical activity can help improve our physical health, boost our mood, and reduce stress and anxiety.

Eat a nutritious diet: Eating a healthy diet that is rich in fruits, vegetables, lean protein, and whole grains can help improve our physical health, boost our mood, and enhance our cognitive function.

Get enough rest: Getting enough sleep is crucial for our physical and mental health. Adults need 7-9 hours of sleep each night to function optimally.

Practice mindfulness and relaxation techniques: Mindfulness and relaxation techniques, such as meditation, deep breathing, and yoga, can help reduce stress and anxiety and promote a sense of calm and relaxation.

Engage in hobbies and interests: Engaging in activities that bring us joy can improve our emotional well-being and enhance our sense of purpose and fulfillment.

Spend time with loved ones: Spending time with loved ones can improve our emotional well-being and strengthen our relationships. It can also provide a sense of support and comfort during difficult times.

Cultivate positive relationships: Cultivating positive relationships with people who share our values, interests, and goals can enhance our emotional well-being and provide a sense of community and belonging.

Practice gratitude: Practicing gratitude can help us focus on the positive aspects of our lives and improve our mental health. We can start by keeping a gratitude journal and writing down things we are grateful for each day.

Set boundaries: Setting boundaries is an essential aspect of self-care. It involves saying no to things that do not serve us and setting limits on the time and energy we give to others.

Take breaks: Taking breaks throughout the day can help us recharge our batteries and improve our productivity. We can take short breaks to stretch, meditate, or take a walk outside.

Conclusion

Self-care is an essential aspect of our overall well-being.

22: THE IMPORTANCE OF SELF-CARE: NURTURING YOUR MIND, BODY, AND SOUL

Taking care of ourselves can help us reduce stress and anxiety, improve our physical health, and enhance our emotional and mental well-being. By engaging in self-care strategies, we can nurture our mind, body, and soul and live a more fulfilling and joyful existence. It is never too late to start taking care of ourselves, and we owe it to ourselves to make self-care a priority in our lives.

23: Connecting with Others: The Role of Community in Achieving Inner Peace

Introduction

Humans are social beings, and our sense of connection and belonging is essential for our overall well-being. While inner peace can be achieved through individual self-help strategies and mindfulness practices, it is equally important to connect with others to achieve a fulfilling and joyful existence. In this chapter, we will explore the role of community in achieving inner peace and discuss various ways to connect with others.

The Importance of Community

Humans have an innate need for social interaction and support. It is through community that we find a sense of belonging, validation, and acceptance. Community also provides a sense of purpose, as we can work together towards common goals and create meaningful relationships.

Research has shown that social isolation and loneliness can have a negative impact on our mental and physical health.

23: CONNECTING WITH OTHERS: THE ROLE OF COMMUNITY IN ACHIEVING INNER PEACE

Studies have linked social isolation to increased risk of depression, anxiety, and even premature death. In contrast, social support has been shown to reduce stress and increase resilience.

Connecting with Others

Connecting with others can take many forms, and there is no one-size-fits-all approach. The key is to find activities and groups that align with your interests and values. Here are some ways to connect with others and build a sense of community:

Volunteer: Volunteering is a great way to give back to the community and connect with like-minded individuals. You can volunteer at a local shelter, hospital, or community center. You can also join a volunteer group or organization that aligns with your values.

Attend Events: Attending events such as concerts, festivals, or community gatherings is a great way to meet new people and connect with your community. Look for events that align with your interests, and don't be afraid to strike up a conversation with someone new.

23: CONNECTING WITH OTHERS: THE ROLE OF COMMUNITY IN ACHIEVING INNER PEACE

Join a Club or Group: Joining a club or group that aligns with your interests is a great way to connect with others who share your passions. Whether it's a book club, sports team, or hobby group, you can build meaningful relationships with like-minded individuals.

Take Classes: Taking classes or workshops is a great way to learn new skills and connect with others. Whether it's a cooking class, yoga workshop, or language course, you can meet new people and expand your horizons.

Attend Support Groups: If you're struggling with a specific issue such as addiction, grief, or mental health, attending a support group can provide a sense of community and understanding. You can find support groups through local organizations or online.

Connect Online: Social media and online communities provide a convenient way to connect with others who share your interests or struggles. However, it's important to be mindful of the content you consume and engage with online, as it can impact your mental health.

Building Strong Relationships

23: CONNECTING WITH OTHERS: THE ROLE OF COMMUNITY IN ACHIEVING INNER PEACE

Connecting with others is only the first step towards building strong relationships. To build meaningful relationships, it's important to be authentic, open, and vulnerable. Here are some tips for building strong relationships:

Practice Active Listening: Active listening involves paying attention to what the other person is saying and responding with empathy and understanding. It's important to give the other person your full attention and avoid distractions such as your phone or other devices.

Communicate Clearly: Clear communication involves expressing your thoughts and feelings in a way that the other person can understand. It's important to be honest and direct, while also being respectful and considerate of the other person's feelings.

Show Empathy: Empathy involves understanding and sharing the feelings of others. It's important to validate the other person's feelings and show that you care about their well-being.

Practice Forgiveness: Forgiveness involves letting go of resentment and anger towards others. It's important to forgive others for their mistakes and to seek forgiveness when you have hurt others.

Be Reliable: Being reliable means following through on commitments and being there for others when they need you. It's important to be dependable and to communicate any changes or issues that may affect your ability to follow through on commitments.

Respect Boundaries: Respecting boundaries involves recognizing and honoring the limits of others. It's important to communicate your own boundaries and to respect the boundaries of others.

Practice Gratitude: Gratitude involves recognizing and appreciating the positive aspects of your relationships. It's important to express gratitude and show appreciation for the people in your life.

The Power of Community for Inner Peace

Connecting with others and building strong relationships can have a profound impact on our sense of inner peace. By building a sense of community, we can find support, validation, and purpose. Community can also provide a sense of belonging, which is essential for our overall well-being.

In addition to the social benefits, community can also provide opportunities for personal growth and spiritual development. By engaging in shared activities and practices, we can deepen our understanding of ourselves and others.

Conclusion

Connecting with others and building a sense of community is essential for our overall well-being and sense of inner peace. By finding ways to connect with others and building strong relationships, we can find support, validation, and purpose. Whether it's through volunteering, attending events, joining a club, or taking classes, there are many ways to connect with others and build a sense of community. Remember to be authentic, open, and vulnerable in your relationships, and practice active listening, clear communication, empathy, forgiveness, reliability, respecting boundaries, and gratitude to build strong relationships.

24: The Benefits of Journaling: Reflection and Self-Discovery

The practice of journaling has been around for centuries and has been used by people from all walks of life as a tool for reflection, self-discovery, and personal growth. Journaling can be a powerful way to understand your thoughts and feelings, explore your dreams and aspirations, and track your progress towards your goals. In this chapter, we will explore the benefits of journaling and how it can help you cultivate inner peace, manage stress and anxiety, and live a more fulfilling life.

Journaling is a simple yet effective way to tap into your inner world and gain insight into your thoughts, emotions, and behaviors. When you write down your thoughts and feelings, you can examine them more objectively and gain a new perspective on your experiences. This can help you identify patterns in your thinking and behavior, recognize your strengths and weaknesses, and make positive changes in your life.

One of the key benefits of journaling is that it can help you manage stress and anxiety. When you write down your worries and fears, you can release them from your mind and re-

duce their power over you. Journaling can also help you
identify the root causes of your stress and anxiety, such as a
challenging work situation, a difficult relationship, or a
health issue. By understanding the sources of your stress,
you can take steps to address them and develop coping
strategies that work for you.

Another benefit of journaling is that it can help you cultivate inner peace and tranquility. When you write down your
thoughts and feelings, you create a space for reflection and
self-awareness. This can help you connect with your inner
wisdom and intuition, and gain a deeper understanding of
your values and priorities. Journaling can also help you cultivate a sense of gratitude and appreciation for the good
things in your life, which can boost your mood and improve
your overall sense of well-being.

Journaling can also be a valuable tool for personal growth
and development. When you reflect on your experiences,
you can identify areas where you want to grow and improve.
You can set goals for yourself and track your progress towards them, which can help you stay motivated and focused. Journaling can also help you develop a deeper un-

derstanding of yourself and your relationships, which can improve your communication skills and enhance your ability to connect with others.

There are many different types of journals that you can use, including gratitude journals, dream journals, and goal-setting journals. Each type of journal has its own unique benefits and can help you achieve different goals. For example, a gratitude journal can help you focus on the positive aspects of your life and cultivate a sense of appreciation and contentment. A dream journal can help you explore your subconscious mind and tap into your creativity and intuition. A goal-setting journal can help you set and achieve meaningful goals that align with your values and aspirations.

In addition to the benefits outlined above, there are many other reasons why journaling can be a valuable practice. For example, journaling can help you:

– Improve your writing skills: Writing regularly can help you become a better writer, which can be a valuable skill in many areas of life.

– Boost your memory: When you write down your thoughts

and experiences, you create a record of your life that you can look back on in the future.

– Reduce symptoms of depression: Journaling can be a helpful tool for people with depression, as it can help them process their emotions and gain a sense of control over their thoughts and feelings.

– Enhance your creativity: Writing can be a powerful way to tap into your imagination and explore new ideas and perspectives.

– Improve your problem-solving skills: Journaling can help you identify solutions to problems and develop strategies for overcoming challenges.

If you are new to journaling, it can be helpful to start with a simple notebook or journal and a pen or pencil. Set aside some time each day or week to write down your thoughts and feelings, and don't worry too much about grammar or spelling. The goal of journaling is not to produce a perfect piece of writing, but to explore your inner world and gain insight into yourself.

24: THE BENEFITS OF JOURNALING: REFLECTION AND SELF-DISCOVERY

To get started, you might consider writing about your day, your goals and aspirations, your relationships, your fears and worries, or anything else that comes to mind. Try to write honestly and authentically, and don't be afraid to explore difficult or uncomfortable emotions. Remember, your journal is a safe space for you to express yourself and reflect on your experiences.

As you continue to journal, you may find that certain themes or patterns emerge in your writing. You may notice recurring thoughts or feelings, or identify areas where you want to make changes in your life. Use these insights as a starting point for further exploration and growth.

It's important to remember that journaling is a personal practice, and there is no right or wrong way to do it. Some people prefer to write long, detailed entries, while others prefer to jot down quick notes or bullet points. Some people prefer to journal in the morning, while others prefer to journal at night. Experiment with different styles and approaches to see what works best for you.

In addition to traditional pen and paper journaling, there are also many digital journaling tools available, such as apps and online platforms. These tools can be convenient and accessible, but it's important to ensure that your digital journal is secure and private.

Overall, journaling can be a powerful tool for cultivating inner peace, managing stress and anxiety, and living a more fulfilling life. By taking the time to reflect on your experiences and explore your inner world, you can gain insight into yourself, improve your well-being, and make positive changes in your life. So why not give it a try? Grab a notebook and pen, or open up a digital journaling app, and start exploring the life-changing power of journaling today!

25: Creativity and Inner Peace: Tapping into Your Creative Potential

Introduction

In today's world, where stress and anxiety have become a part of our daily lives, inner peace has become a rare commodity. We spend most of our time chasing success and material possessions, without realizing that true happiness lies within us. However, we can tap into our creativity to find inner peace and live a fulfilling life. In this chapter, we will explore the relationship between creativity and inner peace and learn how to unlock our creative potential to experience a peaceful existence.

The Link Between Creativity and Inner Peace

Creativity is the act of using our imagination to generate new ideas, concepts, or solutions. It is not just limited to artistic endeavors but can be applied to any aspect of our lives. When we engage in creative activities, we enter a state of flow, which is a mental state where we become fully absorbed in what we are doing, lose track of time, and feel a sense of enjoyment and fulfillment. This state of flow is similar to the state of mindfulness, where we are fully present in the moment and free from distractions.

When we tap into our creativity, we unlock a part of ourselves that is free from the worries and stresses of every-day life. We let go of our fears and doubts and enter a space where we can explore our innermost thoughts and feelings. This space allows us to connect with our true selves and experience a sense of inner peace.

Moreover, studies have shown that engaging in creative activities can have a positive impact on our mental health. Creativity can help reduce stress and anxiety, boost our mood, and increase our overall sense of well-being. By tapping into our creativity, we can experience a sense of calm and contentment that can lead to a more peaceful and ful-filling existence.

Ways to Tap into Your Creative Potential

Start with small steps: Creativity is not something that you can turn on like a switch. It takes time and practice to de-velop your creative potential. Start by incorporating small creative activities into your daily routine, such as doodling, writing, or singing. These small steps can help build your confidence and lead to more significant creative endeavors.

Take risks: Creativity involves taking risks and stepping outside of your comfort zone. Don't be afraid to try something new or different. Embrace the unknown and be open to new possibilities. Taking risks can lead to breakthroughs and new ideas.

Create a dedicated space: Having a dedicated space for your creative endeavors can help you get into the right mindset. It can be a corner of your room or a separate studio space. Make sure that your space is clutter-free and has everything you need to get started.

Find inspiration: Inspiration can come from anywhere. It can be in nature, a book, or a work of art. Find what inspires you and use it as a starting point for your creative endeavors. Surround yourself with things that inspire you, such as quotes or images, to keep you motivated.

Collaborate: Collaborating with others can help spark new ideas and provide a fresh perspective. Find people who share your interests and passions and work together on a project. Collaboration can help you grow as a creative and expand your horizons.

Practice mindfulness: Mindfulness can help you tap into your creative potential by allowing you to focus on the present moment. When you are mindful, you are fully present in what you are doing, free from distractions and worries. This state of mindfulness can help you access your inner creativity and find a sense of inner peace.

Conclusion

Creativity and inner peace are interconnected. When we tap into our creativity, we enter a state of flow and let go of our worries and stresses. We can experience a sense of inner peace and fulfillment that can lead to a more joyful existence. By incorporating small steps, taking risks, creating a dedicated space, finding inspiration, collaborating with others, and practicing mindfulness, we can unlock our creative potential and experience the life-changing power of inner peace.

In addition to the tips mentioned above, there are many other ways to tap into your creative potential. Some people find that taking walks in nature or practicing meditation can help them access their inner creativity. Others find that listening to music or playing an instrument can help them tap into their creative flow.

It's important to remember that everyone's creative process is different. Some people work best in solitude, while others thrive in a group setting. Some people prefer to work in the morning, while others are more productive in the evening. Experiment with different approaches and find what works best for you.

Finally, it's important to be patient with yourself. Developing your creative potential takes time and practice. Don't be discouraged if your first attempts don't turn out as you hoped. Keep experimenting and learning, and you'll eventually find your own creative voice.

In conclusion, creativity and inner peace are essential components of a fulfilling and joyful existence. By tapping into our creative potential, we can experience a sense of calm and contentment that can help us navigate the stresses of everyday life. So, start small, take risks, find inspiration, collaborate with others, practice mindfulness, and be patient. Your journey to inner peace and creativity begins today.

26: Finding Your Spiritual Path: Exploring Different Belief Systems

Introduction

We live in a world that is diverse in every way possible. From the food we eat, to the clothes we wear, and the languages we speak, there is no denying that we are all unique in our own ways. One of the biggest aspects of this diversity is the different belief systems that people follow. With so many religions and spiritual practices in the world, it can be overwhelming to find the right path that resonates with you. However, this chapter is dedicated to helping you explore the different belief systems and find your spiritual path.

Understanding the Different Belief Systems

Before we dive into the various belief systems, it is essential to understand that there are two major types of beliefs: monotheistic and polytheistic. Monotheistic beliefs are those that believe in one God, while polytheistic beliefs are those that believe in many gods. With that said, let's explore some of the most popular religions and spiritual practices in the world.

26: FINDING YOUR SPIRITUAL PATH: EXPLORING DIF-FERENT BELIEF SYSTEMS

Christianity

Christianity is a monotheistic religion that follows the teachings of Jesus Christ. It is the most popular religion in the world, with over 2.4 billion followers. Christians believe in one God who created the universe and sent his son, Jesus Christ, to save humanity from sin. Christians believe in the Bible as the word of God and attend church to worship and pray.

Islam

Islam is a monotheistic religion that follows the teachings of the prophet Muhammad. It is the second-largest religion in the world, with over 1.8 billion followers. Muslims believe in one God, Allah, who created the universe and sent his prophet Muhammad to deliver his message. Muslims believe in the Quran as the word of God and attend the mosque to worship and pray.

Hinduism

Hinduism is a polytheistic religion that originated in India. It has over one billion followers worldwide. Hindus believe in many gods and goddesses who control different aspects of life. They believe in karma, reincarnation, and the ulti-mate goal of reaching enlightenment. Hindus worship in temples and perform various rituals and ceremonies.

Buddhism

Buddhism is a non-theistic religion that originated in India. It has over 500 million followers worldwide. Buddhists be-lieve in the teachings of Siddhartha Gautama, also known as the Buddha. They believe in the Four Noble Truths and the Eightfold Path as the way to achieve enlightenment. Buddhists meditate to calm their minds and develop inner peace.

Taoism

Taoism is a non-theistic religion that originated in China. It has over 20 million followers worldwide. Taoists believe in the Tao, which is the way of the universe. They believe in yin and yang, the balance of opposites, and the Tao Te Ching as their holy book. Taoists practice meditation, qi-gong, and other physical exercises to achieve inner peace.

26: FINDING YOUR SPIRITUAL PATH: EXPLORING DIFFERENT BELIEF SYSTEMS

Wicca

Wicca is a neopagan religion that originated in England. It has over one million followers worldwide. Wiccans believe in the worship of nature and the goddess and god. They practice witchcraft, perform spells, and celebrate the cycles of the moon and the seasons. Wiccans create their own rituals and ceremonies.

Scientology

Scientology is a non-theistic religion that originated in the United States. It has over 500,000 followers worldwide. Scientologists believe in the power of the mind and the soul. They practice auditing, which is a form of therapy that helps individuals overcome their negative emotions and thoughts. Scientologists also believe in reincarnation and the ultimate goal of achieving spiritual enlightenment.

Judaism

Judaism is a monotheistic religion that originated in the Middle East. It has over 14 million followers worldwide. Jews believe in one God who created the universe and sent prophets to deliver his message. They believe in the Torah as their holy book and attend synagogue to worship and pray. Jews also celebrate various holidays and perform rituals and ceremonies.

Sikhism

Sikhism is a monotheistic religion that originated in India. It has over 25 million followers worldwide. Sikhs believe in one God, who is the same for all religions. They believe in the teachings of the ten Sikh gurus and the Guru Granth Sahib as their holy book. Sikhs attend the gurdwara to worship and pray and also engage in charitable activities.

Confucianism

Confucianism is a non-theistic religion that originated in China. It has over 6 million followers worldwide. Confucianists believe in the importance of education, social harmony, and the cultivation of virtue. They follow the teachings of Confucius, which include the Five Classics and the Four Books. Confucianists also practice ancestor worship.

Finding Your Spiritual Path

26: FINDING YOUR SPIRITUAL PATH: EXPLORING DIFFERENT BELIEF SYSTEMS

With so many religions and spiritual practices to choose from, it can be challenging to find the right path that resonates with you. Here are some tips to help you find your spiritual path:

Explore: Take the time to explore different religions and spiritual practices. Attend services, read books, and talk to people who practice different beliefs. This will help you gain a better understanding of what each religion or practice entails.

Reflect: After exploring different religions and practices, take some time to reflect on what resonates with you. Consider your values, beliefs, and goals in life. Think about what feels right to you and what aligns with your inner self.

Experiment: Once you have narrowed down your choices, experiment with different practices. Attend different services, meditate, pray, or perform rituals. This will help you experience the practices firsthand and determine if they are right for you.

Seek guidance: If you are still struggling to find your spiritual path, seek guidance from a spiritual leader or mentor.

26: FINDING YOUR SPIRITUAL PATH: EXPLORING DIFFERENT BELIEF SYSTEMS

They can help you explore different beliefs and practices and provide support and guidance as you embark on your spiritual journey.

Conclusion

In conclusion, finding your spiritual path is a personal journey that requires exploration, reflection, and experimentation. There is no one-size-fits-all solution, and it may take time to find the right path that resonates with you. Remember to keep an open mind and be patient with yourself as you navigate this journey. With dedication and perseverance, you can find inner peace and live a fulfilling and joyful existence.

27: The Power of Prayer: Connecting with a Higher Power

The power of prayer is an incredible force that can connect us with a higher power, fill us with positive energy, and help us overcome any challenge that we may face in life. Prayer is not just a religious practice, but it is a spiritual practice that has been embraced by people of different faiths and beliefs for centuries. It is a way to communicate with the divine and express our gratitude, hopes, and fears.

Prayer is a form of meditation that helps us focus our thoughts and intentions on what we truly desire in life. It is a way to access the power of the universe and manifest our desires. When we pray, we are not just asking for something; we are setting our intentions and sending out positive energy into the world. This positive energy then attracts more positivity, and we begin to see the results of our prayers manifesting in our lives.

One of the most important things to remember about prayer is that it is not just about asking for things. Prayer is also about expressing gratitude for the blessings in our lives, connecting with a higher power, and seeking guidance and wisdom. When we pray with a sincere heart, we open ourselves up to receiving blessings and guidance from the universe.

Prayer can take many different forms, from traditional religious prayers to personal affirmations and mantras. It is up to each individual to find the form of prayer that resonates with them and their beliefs. Some people find comfort in reciting traditional prayers from their religious traditions, while others prefer to create their own prayers or meditate on a particular intention or mantra.

Regardless of the form of prayer, the most important thing is to approach it with sincerity and an open heart. When we pray, we should do so with the intention of connecting with a higher power and seeking guidance and wisdom. We should also approach prayer with a spirit of gratitude, acknowledging the blessings in our lives and expressing our appreciation for them.

In addition to its spiritual benefits, prayer has been shown to have a positive impact on our physical and mental well-being. Studies have found that regular prayer and meditation can reduce stress and anxiety, lower blood pressure, improve immune function, and even enhance brain function.

If you are new to prayer, it may take some time to find the form of prayer that resonates with you. You may also find it helpful to seek guidance from a spiritual leader or teacher, or to join a prayer group or community. Whatever form of prayer you choose, remember that it is a powerful tool that can help you connect with a higher power, find peace and fulfillment, and manifest your desires in life.

28: Connecting with the Universe: The Role of Astrology and Tarot

Introduction

Astrology and Tarot are two ancient practices that have been used for centuries to gain insights into the workings of the universe and our place in it. They both provide a framework for understanding the forces that shape our lives and offer a language for communicating with the divine. In this chapter, we will explore the role of astrology and tarot in our quest for inner peace, and how we can use these practices to connect with the universe and tap into its transformative power.

Astrology

Astrology is a system of divination that uses the positions of the planets, stars, and other celestial bodies to gain insights into human behavior and personality traits. It is based on the idea that the movements and alignments of these heavenly bodies have a profound influence on our lives and shape our destiny.

The study of astrology can be complex and nuanced, but at

its core, it involves understanding the twelve zodiac signs, the planets that rule them, and the relationships between them. Each zodiac sign represents a different set of personality traits and characteristics, and the positions of the planets in relation to the signs can provide valuable insights into our strengths, weaknesses, and potential paths in life.

One of the most popular applications of astrology is the birth chart, which is a map of the positions of the planets at the time of a person's birth. By analyzing the birth chart, astrologers can gain a deep understanding of a person's personality, relationships, career path, and life purpose. This information can be incredibly valuable for individuals seeking to understand themselves and navigate life's challenges.

Astrology can also be used for forecasting, by examining the movement of the planets and predicting how they will affect different areas of our lives. For example, an astrologer might predict a time of heightened creativity or emotional intensity based on the position of the planets.

While some may be skeptical of astrology's validity, it is important to remember that the practice has been used for thousands of years across many different cultures. Whether or not one believes in its accuracy, astrology can provide a powerful tool for self-reflection and self-discovery.

Tarot

Tarot is another ancient divination tool that uses a deck of 78 cards to gain insights into the past, present, and future. Each card has a unique meaning and symbolism, and the cards are arranged in a spread to create a narrative that can be interpreted to provide guidance and clarity.

Tarot has its roots in medieval Europe, where it was originally used as a game before evolving into a tool for divination. The Tarot deck consists of four suits (wands, cups, swords, and pentacles) and a set of twenty-two cards known as the Major Arcana. Each card in the Major Arcana represents a powerful archetype or universal concept, such as the Fool, the Magician, or the Death card.

When using Tarot for divination, a reader will often ask a question or set an intention before shuffling the deck and drawing cards. The cards that are drawn will then be interpreted in the context of the question or intention, providing insights into the situation at hand and potential paths forward.

While Tarot can be used for forecasting, it is important to remember that it is not a tool for predicting the future with absolute certainty. Rather, it provides a lens through which we can examine our current situation and gain new perspectives and insights. Tarot can be a powerful tool for introspection, self-discovery, and personal growth.

Connecting with the Universe

Both astrology and Tarot offer powerful tools for connecting with the universe and gaining insights into our place in it. By examining the movements of the planets and the symbolism of the Tarot cards, we can tap into the forces that shape our lives and gain a deeper understanding of ourselves and the world around us.

29: The Importance of Ritual and Ceremony: Honoring Life Transitions

As human beings, we all experience transitions in our lives, both positive and negative. These transitions can range from major life events such as marriage, the birth of a child, or the loss of a loved one, to smaller transitions such as changing jobs or moving to a new city. Regardless of the size of the transition, it is important to honor it and recognize its significance in our lives. One powerful way to do this is through ritual and ceremony.

Rituals and ceremonies have been a part of human culture for thousands of years. They have been used to mark important events, celebrate milestones, and provide a sense of connection and belonging. These traditions vary across different cultures and religions, but they all share a common purpose: to bring people together and provide a meaningful way to honor and remember important life transitions.

In our modern world, we have lost touch with many of these traditional rituals and ceremonies. We often rush through life, moving from one event to the next without taking the

time to pause and reflect. As a result, we can feel disconnected, anxious, and unfulfilled. By incorporating rituals and
ceremonies into our lives, we can create a sense of connection and meaning, and experience greater peace and fulfillment.

One of the most powerful ways to honor life transitions is
through a ritual or ceremony. This can be as simple or as
elaborate as you like. The important thing is to make it
meaningful and personal. Here are a few examples of how
you can incorporate ritual and ceremony into your life:

Creating a Sacred Space: One way to honor a life transition
is to create a sacred space. This can be a physical space in
your home or a special location outside. Fill the space with
objects that have special meaning to you, such as candles,
crystals, or photographs. Take time each day to sit in this
space and reflect on the transition you are going through.

Writing a Letter: Writing a letter to yourself or to someone
else can be a powerful way to honor a life transition. Use
this letter to reflect on your journey so far and express your
hopes and dreams for the future. You can choose to keep
the letter private, or you can read it aloud as part of a cere-

mony.

Planting a Tree: Planting a tree can be a powerful way to symbolize a new beginning or a fresh start. Choose a tree that has special meaning to you, and take the time to plant it in a special location. You can then return to this location each year to reflect on your journey and watch the tree grow.

Holding a Ceremony: Holding a ceremony can be a powerful way to honor a life transition. This can be a small, intimate gathering or a larger event with friends and family. Choose rituals or activities that have special meaning to you, such as lighting candles, singing songs, or sharing stories.

Regardless of the specific ritual or ceremony you choose, the important thing is to take the time to honor the transition you are going through. By creating a meaningful and personal way to mark this event, you can experience greater peace, connection, and fulfillment in your life.

In addition to honoring life transitions, rituals and ceremonies can also be used to create a sense of routine and stability in our lives. Many of us feel overwhelmed by the pace of modern life, and struggle to find a sense of balance and calm. By incorporating regular rituals and ceremonies into our lives, we can create a sense of structure and routine that can help us feel more grounded and centered.

Some examples of daily rituals that can help promote a sense of peace and calm include meditation, yoga, journaling, or taking a walk in nature. These activities can be done alone or with others, and can be customized to fit your individual needs and preferences.

In addition to daily rituals, there are also seasonal rituals and ceremonies that can be incorporated into our lives. Many cultures and religions have traditions that are tied to specific times of year, such as the changing of the seasons or the cycles of the moon. By participating in these rituals and ceremonies, we can connect to something larger than ourselves and experience a sense of belonging and community.

For example, many cultures celebrate the winter solstice, the longest night of the year, as a time of reflection and renewal. This can be done by lighting candles, creating a sacred space, or participating in a community ceremony. Similarly, the spring equinox is often celebrated as a time of new beginnings and growth, and can be honored through planting a garden or participating in a spring cleaning ritual.

By incorporating these seasonal rituals and ceremonies into our lives, we can experience a sense of connection to the natural world and to the larger cycles of life. This can help us feel more grounded, centered, and at peace.

Finally, it is important to recognize that rituals and ceremonies are not a panacea for all of life's challenges. While they can be a powerful tool for promoting inner peace and connection, they are not a substitute for seeking professional help when needed. If you are struggling with anxiety, depression, or other mental health challenges, it is important to seek the support of a qualified therapist or counselor.

In conclusion, rituals and ceremonies can be a powerful tool for promoting inner peace, connection, and fulfillment in our lives. By taking the time to honor life transitions, create a sense of routine and stability, and connect to something larger than ourselves, we can experience a greater sense of meaning and purpose. Whether you choose to incorporate daily rituals into your life, participate in seasonal ceremonies, or create your own unique traditions, the important thing is to find practices that resonate with you and help you feel more connected and at peace.

30: Mindful Eating: Nourishing Your Body and Mind

As human beings, we have a complex relationship with food. We need food to survive, but we also use it for comfort, celebration, and pleasure. Eating can be a source of joy and nourishment, but it can also become a source of stress, anxiety, and guilt. Mindful eating is a powerful tool that can help us transform our relationship with food and cultivate a more peaceful and positive attitude towards ourselves and the world.

In this chapter, we will explore the concept of mindful eating, its benefits, and practical strategies to incorporate it into your life. We will also examine the connection between food and emotions, and how mindful eating can help you manage your feelings and cultivate a deeper sense of inner peace.

What is Mindful Eating?

Mindful eating is the practice of paying attention to the present moment while eating, without judgment or distraction. It involves using all of our senses to fully experience the taste, smell, texture, and appearance of the food we are eating. It also involves being aware of our physical sensations, emotions, and thoughts related to eating, without reacting to them or being overwhelmed by them.

Mindful eating is not a diet or a restrictive eating plan. It is a way of approaching food with curiosity, openness, and kindness, and developing a more intuitive and respectful relationship with our bodies and our environment. Mindful eating is not about perfection or control, but about self-awareness and self-care.

The Benefits of Mindful Eating

The benefits of mindful eating are numerous and far-reaching. Research has shown that mindful eating can:

Help you manage your weight: By paying attention to your hunger and fullness cues, and eating when you are hungry and stopping when you are full, you can prevent overeating and reduce emotional eating.

Improve your digestion: By chewing your food slowly and mindfully, you can improve your digestion and reduce bloating, indigestion, and other digestive problems.

Reduce stress and anxiety: By eating mindfully, you can reduce stress and anxiety related to food and eating, and develop a more positive and peaceful attitude towards yourself and the world.

Enhance your enjoyment of food: By fully experiencing the taste, smell, and texture of the food you are eating, you can enhance your enjoyment of food and develop a deeper appreciation for the variety and richness of the culinary world.

Increase your self-awareness: By paying attention to your physical sensations, emotions, and thoughts related to eating, you can increase your self-awareness and develop a deeper understanding of your body and your needs.

Practical Strategies for Mindful Eating

Now that you understand the benefits of mindful eating, let's explore some practical strategies to incorporate it into your life:

Slow down: One of the key principles of mindful eating is slowing down and savoring each bite. Take your time to chew your food slowly and mindfully, and pay attention to the flavors and textures of the food.

Eat without distractions: Avoid eating while watching TV, browsing your phone, or working on your computer. Eating with distractions can lead to mindless eating and overeating.

Pay attention to your hunger and fullness cues: Tune in to your body and notice when you are hungry and when you are full. Eat when you are hungry and stop when you are full, even if there is food left on your plate.

Practice gratitude: Take a moment before you start eating to express gratitude for the food and the people who made it possible. This can help you cultivate a sense of appreciation and joy towards your food.

Listen to your body: Pay attention to your physical sensations, emotions, and thoughts related to eating. Notice any cravings, urges, or emotions that arise, and observe them without judgment or reaction.

Choose healthy and nourishing foods: Practice mindful grocery shopping: Before you go to the grocery store, make a list of the foods that you need, and choose foods that will nourish your body and mind. Avoid buying foods that you know are unhealthy or that trigger negative emotions.

Cook mindfully: When you are cooking, try to be present in the moment and focus on the task at hand. Enjoy the process of preparing the food and appreciate the flavors and aromas of the ingredients.

Practice portion control: Use smaller plates and bowls to help you control your portions. Pay attention to your hunger and fullness cues, and stop eating when you are satisfied.

Cultivate self-compassion: If you slip up and eat mindlessly or overeat, don't beat yourself up. Instead, practice self-compassion and self-forgiveness, and use it as an opportunity to learn and grow.

Food and Emotions

Food and emotions are closely linked, and many of us use food as a way to cope with stress, anxiety, and negative emotions. We may turn to comfort foods when we feel sad or lonely, or use food as a way to celebrate or reward ourselves.

However, this can lead to a cycle of emotional eating, where we use food as a way to numb our emotions or distract ourselves from our problems. This can ultimately lead to guilt, shame, and negative self-talk, which can further fuel the cycle of emotional eating.

Mindful eating can help us break this cycle by helping us become more aware of our emotions and our relationship with food. By paying attention to our physical sensations, emotions, and thoughts related to eating, we can begin to identify the triggers and patterns of emotional eating, and develop more effective and healthy ways to cope with our emotions.

Conclusion

Mindful eating is a powerful tool that can help us cultivate a more peaceful and positive relationship with food and our bodies. By practicing mindfulness while eating, we can develop a deeper appreciation for the richness and variety of the culinary world, while also nourishing our bodies and minds.

Through mindful eating, we can also learn to manage our emotions and develop a more intuitive and respectful relationship with our bodies and our environment. With practice and patience, mindful eating can become a natural and joyful part of our daily lives, and help us live a more fulfilling and joyful existence.

31: The Connection between Sleep and Inner Peace: Tips for Better Sleep

Introduction

Sleep is a crucial aspect of our physical and mental well-being. It is the time when our body repairs itself, our brain consolidates memories, and our emotions regulate themselves. Yet, in our fast-paced, over-stimulating modern world, many of us struggle to get the restful sleep we need. Insomnia, sleep disturbances, and sleep-related disorders are on the rise, leading to a host of physical and mental health problems. In this chapter, we will explore the connection between sleep and inner peace, and provide tips for better sleep that can help you achieve a more fulfilling and joyful existence.

The Importance of Sleep for Inner Peace

Inner peace is a state of mind characterized by a sense of calm, clarity, and contentment. It is the opposite of anxiety, stress, and negativity. When we are well-rested, we are more likely to experience inner peace, because sleep helps regulate our emotions and reduce stress. When we are sleep-deprived, on the other hand, we are more likely to be irritable, anxious, and negative.

Sleep also plays a crucial role in our physical health. Chronic sleep deprivation has been linked to a host of health problems, including obesity, diabetes, cardiovascular disease, and weakened immune function. Getting enough restful sleep is essential for maintaining good physical health and overall well-being.

Tips for Better Sleep

Create a Sleep-Conducive Environment

The first step to getting better sleep is creating a sleep-conducive environment. Your bedroom should be cool, dark, and quiet. Use blackout curtains or an eye mask to block out any light, and earplugs or white noise to mask any sound. Make sure your bed is comfortable and supportive, and invest in high-quality sheets and pillows.

Establish a Sleep Routine

Establishing a consistent sleep routine is one of the most effective ways to improve the quality of your sleep. Go to bed and wake up at the same time every day, even on weekends. This helps regulate your body's circadian rhythm, which governs your sleep-wake cycle. Avoid napping during the day, as this can disrupt your nighttime sleep.

Limit Screen Time Before Bed

The blue light emitted by electronic screens can interfere with your body's production of melatonin, a hormone that helps regulate sleep. Avoid using electronic devices for at least an hour before bedtime. Instead, engage in relaxing activities like reading a book, taking a bath, or meditating.

Exercise Regularly

Regular exercise has been shown to improve the quality of sleep, especially when done early in the day. Aim for at least 30 minutes of moderate exercise most days of the week. However, avoid vigorous exercise in the evening, as this can interfere with your ability to fall asleep.

Manage Stress

Stress is a major contributor to sleep problems. Learning to manage stress can help you sleep better. Engage in stress-reducing activities like yoga, meditation, or deep breathing exercises. Write down your worries and concerns before bed to help clear your mind.

Avoid Stimulants

Avoid caffeine, nicotine, and alcohol in the hours leading up to bedtime. These substances can interfere with your ability to fall asleep and stay asleep. If you must have caffeine, limit your intake to the morning hours.

Try Natural Remedies

Natural remedies like herbal teas, aromatherapy, and relaxation techniques can help promote better sleep. Chamomile, valerian root, and lavender are all known for their calming properties. Experiment with different remedies to find what works best for you.

Conclusion

Getting enough restful sleep is essential for achieving inner peace and overall well-being. By creating a sleep-conducive environment, establishing a sleep routine, limiting screen time before bed, exercising regularly, managing stress, avoiding stimulants, and trying natural remedies, you can improve the quality and quantity of your sleep. Remember that getting better sleep is a process that takes time and effort. It may take several weeks or even months to see significant improvements in your sleep habits. Be patient and persistent, and don't give up if you experience setbacks along the way.

In addition to these tips, it's important to seek professional help if you are experiencing chronic sleep problems or sleep-related disorders. A sleep specialist can help identify the underlying causes of your sleep disturbances and provide personalized recommendations for treatment.

Ultimately, improving the quality of your sleep is one of the most effective ways to achieve inner peace and a fulfilling, joyful existence. When you are well-rested, you are better equipped to handle life's challenges with calmness, clarity, and resilience. So, prioritize your sleep, and watch as your inner peace and overall well-being flourish.

32: Mindful Movement: Finding Peace through Exercise

In our busy and fast-paced world, finding time to exercise can be a challenge. But exercise is crucial for our physical, mental, and emotional well-being. It not only helps us stay fit and healthy, but it also reduces stress, anxiety, and depression, boosts our mood, and improves our self-esteem. However, not all exercises are created equal when it comes to promoting inner peace. Some can be stressful, competitive, and even harmful to our bodies and minds. That's why it's essential to choose the right type of exercise that aligns with our values, goals, and temperament.

One type of exercise that has gained popularity in recent years is mindful movement. Mindful movement combines the benefits of physical activity with the principles of mindfulness, such as awareness, non-judgment, and presence. It involves moving our bodies in a mindful and intentional way, paying attention to our breath, sensations, and thoughts, and cultivating a sense of calm, focus, and joy. Mindful movement encompasses a variety of practices, from yoga and tai chi to dance and hiking, and can be adapted to different fitness levels and preferences.

32: MINDFUL MOVEMENT: FINDING PEACE THROUGH EXERCISE

One of the main benefits of mindful movement is its ability to reduce stress and anxiety. When we engage in physical activity, our body releases endorphins, which are natural mood-boosters and painkillers. Endorphins also reduce the production of stress hormones, such as cortisol, that can damage our immune system, impair our memory, and increase our risk of chronic diseases. By adding mindfulness to the mix, we can amplify the stress-reducing effects of exercise. Mindfulness helps us shift our focus from worries, distractions, and negative thoughts to the present moment, where we can find peace, gratitude, and joy.

Another benefit of mindful movement is its ability to improve our posture, balance, and flexibility. When we sit or stand for long periods, our muscles and joints can become stiff and sore, leading to discomfort, tension, and fatigue. Mindful movement helps us stretch and strengthen our muscles, improve our range of motion, and enhance our body awareness. By tuning in to our body sensations and movements, we can detect and correct imbalances, asymmetries, and misalignments that can lead to injuries and chronic pain. Moreover, by practicing mindfulness while moving, we can prevent mindless habits, such as slouching, clenching, and holding our breath, that can exacerbate physical and emotional stress.

Mindful movement can also boost our cognitive function and creativity. When we engage in physical activity, our brain receives more oxygen and nutrients, which can enhance our memory, focus, and mental clarity. By adding mindfulness to the mix, we can further enhance our cognitive abilities. Mindfulness helps us train our attention, strengthen our working memory, and enhance our executive functions, such as decision-making, problem-solving, and planning. Moreover, by engaging in mindful movement, we can tap into our creativity and intuition, as we explore new movements, postures, and expressions that can expand our range of possibilities and perspectives.

One of the most significant benefits of mindful movement is its ability to connect us with our inner self and others. When we engage in physical activity, we can experience a sense of flow, or "being in the zone," where our actions and awareness merge, and time seems to fly. By adding mindfulness to the mix, we can deepen our sense of connection and empathy. Mindfulness helps us cultivate a sense of presence and acceptance, where we can appreciate ourselves and others without judgment or comparison. Moreover, by engaging in mindful movement with others, we can create a sense of community and belonging, where we can share our experiences, support each other, and learn from each other's perspectives.

To enjoy the benefits of mindful movement, we don't need to be experts or join fancy classes. We can start with simple practices that suit our interests and abilities, and gradually build on them. Here are some examples of mindful movement practices that we can incorporate into our daily routine:

Yoga: Yoga is a popular mindful movement practice that combines physical postures, breath control, and meditation. Yoga can help us improve our flexibility, strength, and balance, while reducing stress, anxiety, and depression. There are many types of yoga, from gentle and restorative to vigorous and challenging, and we can choose the ones that match our goals and preferences. We can practice yoga at home, with the help of online videos, books, or apps, or join a yoga studio or gym that offers yoga classes.

32: MINDFUL MOVEMENT: FINDING PEACE THROUGH EXERCISE

Walking: Walking is a simple yet powerful mindful movement practice that can help us reduce stress, improve our cardiovascular health, and enhance our mood. Walking can be done anywhere, anytime, and doesn't require any special equipment or skills. To make walking more mindful, we can pay attention to our breath, sensations, and surroundings, and try to walk at a moderate pace that allows us to feel comfortable and relaxed.

Dancing: Dancing is a fun and creative mindful movement practice that can help us express ourselves, connect with our emotions, and release tension. Dancing can be done alone or with others, and can involve different styles and genres, such as salsa, hip hop, or ballroom. To make dancing more mindful, we can focus on our body movements, rhythm, and music, and let go of self-consciousness or performance pressure.

Tai Chi: Tai Chi is a gentle and graceful mindful movement practice that originated in China and has gained popularity around the world. Tai Chi involves slow and fluid movements, combined with breathing and visualization techniques, and can help us reduce stress, improve our balance, and enhance our immune system. Tai Chi can be practiced in groups or individually, and doesn't require any special equipment or clothing.

Hiking: Hiking is a mindful movement practice that combines physical activity with nature immersion. Hiking can help us reduce stress, improve our cardiovascular health, and enhance our appreciation of the natural world. To make hiking more mindful, we can pay attention to our breath, sensations, and environment, and try to connect with the sights, sounds, and smells around us.

In conclusion, mindful movement can be a powerful tool for finding peace and improving our overall well-being. By combining physical activity with mindfulness, we can reduce stress, anxiety, and negativity, improve our physical health, cognitive function, and creativity, and enhance our sense of connection and empathy. Mindful movement practices can be adapted to our preferences, abilities, and lifestyles, and can be incorporated into our daily routine in various ways. By practicing mindful movement regularly, we can transform our body, mind, and spirit, and embrace a more fulfilling and joyful existence.

33: Mindful Parenting: Nurturing Your Children and Yourself

As a parent, you want the best for your child. You want them to grow up to be happy, healthy, and successful. But being a parent is not an easy job. It can be overwhelming, stressful, and sometimes frustrating. It's important to find ways to nurture your children and yourself. One way to do that is through mindful parenting.

Mindful parenting is about being present and engaged with your child in a non-judgmental way. It's about tuning into your child's needs and emotions, and responding with kindness and compassion. It's also about taking care of yourself, so that you have the energy and resources to be a good parent.

In this chapter, we'll explore the principles of mindful parenting and offer practical tips for incorporating mindfulness into your parenting style.

Principles of Mindful Parenting

Be present and attentive. Mindful parenting starts with being present and attentive to your child. This means putting aside distractions and focusing on your child in the moment. It means listening to your child with an open mind and heart, and responding with empathy and understanding.

Practice non-judgment. Mindful parenting is about accepting your child for who they are, without judgment or criticism. It's about recognizing that your child is unique and has their own strengths and challenges. It's also about being compassionate and patient with yourself as a parent, recognizing that you're doing the best you can.

Cultivate self-awareness. Mindful parenting involves being aware of your own thoughts, feelings, and reactions. It means taking the time to reflect on your own experiences as a parent, and being willing to make changes when necessary. It also means being mindful of your own self-care, so that you can be a positive and supportive presence for your child.

Practice empathy and compassion. Mindful parenting means putting yourself in your child's shoes and seeing the world from their perspective. It means being empathetic and compassionate, and responding to your child with kindness and understanding. It also means modeling these qualities for your child, so that they can learn to be empathetic and compassionate themselves.

Foster a sense of connection. Mindful parenting is about fostering a sense of connection and intimacy with your child. It means taking the time to play, laugh, and have fun with your child. It also means being available and responsive to your child's needs, and creating a safe and secure environment where your child feels loved and supported.

Practical Tips for Mindful Parenting

Practice mindfulness meditation. Mindfulness meditation is a powerful tool for cultivating mindfulness and self-awareness. It can help you become more present and attentive, and better able to respond to your child's needs. You can start with just a few minutes a day, and gradually increase the time as you become more comfortable with the practice.

Use mindfulness in everyday activities. You can incorporate mindfulness into your everyday activities, such as eating, walking, and playing with your child. This means being fully present and engaged in the activity, and noticing your thoughts and feelings without judgment.

Practice active listening. Active listening means giving your child your full attention when they're speaking to you. It means listening with an open mind and heart, and responding with empathy and understanding. It also means being patient and allowing your child to express themselves fully, without interrupting or judging.

Create a daily routine. Creating a daily routine can help you and your child feel more grounded and centered. This can include regular meal times, play times, and bedtimes. It can also include time for self-care, such as exercise, meditation, or a relaxing bath.

Take care of yourself. Mindful parenting starts with taking care of yourself. This means making time for self-care activities that nourish your mind, body, and spirit. This can include exercise, meditation, reading, spending time in nature, or doing something creative. Taking care of yourself also means being kind and compassionate towards yourself, and recognizing that you're doing the best you can as a parent.

Practice positive discipline. Positive discipline is about setting clear boundaries and expectations for your child, while also emphasizing positive reinforcement and empathy. It's about helping your child learn from their mistakes, rather than punishing or shaming them. Positive discipline can help build your child's self-esteem and sense of responsibility, while also strengthening your relationship with them.

Practice gratitude. Practicing gratitude can help shift your focus from what's wrong to what's right in your life. It can also help you appreciate the small moments of joy and connection with your child. You can practice gratitude by keeping a gratitude journal, or simply taking a moment each day to reflect on what you're grateful for.

Seek support. Mindful parenting can be challenging at times, and it's important to seek support when you need it. This can include reaching out to friends or family for help, joining a parenting support group, or seeing a therapist. Seeking support can help you feel less alone, and provide you with tools and resources to navigate the ups and downs of parenting.

Conclusion

33: MINDFUL PARENTING: NURTURING YOUR CHILDREN AND YOURSELF

Mindful parenting is a powerful practice that can help you and your child thrive. It's about being present, non-judgmental, and compassionate towards yourself and your child. It's about cultivating self-awareness and empathy, and creating a sense of connection and intimacy with your child. By incorporating mindfulness into your parenting style, you can build a strong and loving relationship with your child, and help them develop the skills they need to succeed in life.

34: Finding Peace at Work: Strategies for a More Fulfilling Career

Introduction

In today's fast-paced and demanding world, it can be difficult to find peace in our daily lives, especially in our professional lives. Work can be a significant source of stress, anxiety, and negativity, impacting our mental and physical health, relationships, and overall well-being.

However, finding inner peace at work is not impossible. With the right mindset, strategies, and practices, we can cultivate a more fulfilling and joyful career, one that aligns with our values and purpose, and helps us achieve our goals and aspirations.

In this chapter, we will explore some of the most effective ways to find peace at work, from developing a positive attitude and mindset to setting boundaries, managing stress, and embracing mindfulness and spiritual practices.

Develop a Positive Attitude and Mindset

34: FINDING PEACE AT WORK: STRATEGIES FOR A MORE FULFILLING CAREER

One of the most important steps to finding peace at work is developing a positive attitude and mindset. This means focusing on the good things in our job, such as the opportunities to learn and grow, the sense of accomplishment and contribution, and the relationships we build with our colleagues and clients.

To develop a positive attitude, it's essential to practice gratitude and appreciation. Take some time each day to reflect on the things you are grateful for, such as your skills and talents, the support of your family and friends, and the opportunities that come your way. You can write them down in a journal or share them with a trusted friend or mentor.

Another key to a positive mindset is reframing negative thoughts and beliefs. Instead of seeing challenges and setbacks as insurmountable obstacles, try to view them as opportunities to learn and improve. Focus on solutions rather than problems, and don't let fear and self-doubt hold you back from pursuing your goals and dreams.

Set Boundaries and Prioritize Self-Care

Another important aspect of finding peace at work is setting boundaries and prioritizing self-care. This means learning to say "no" to unreasonable demands and expectations, delegating tasks, and taking breaks and time off when necessary.

Setting boundaries is essential for maintaining our physical, emotional, and mental health. It helps us avoid burnout and exhaustion, and enables us to be more present and focused when we are at work. To set boundaries effectively, it's essential to communicate clearly and assertively with our supervisors, colleagues, and clients. Let them know what you can and cannot do, and negotiate reasonable deadlines and expectations.

Self-care is also crucial for finding peace at work. It means taking care of our physical, emotional, and spiritual needs, such as getting enough sleep, eating healthy foods, exercising regularly, and practicing relaxation and stress-management techniques. It also means taking time for hobbies, interests, and relationships outside of work, to recharge and renew our energy and motivation.

Manage Stress and Emotions

34: FINDING PEACE AT WORK: STRATEGIES FOR A MORE FULFILLING CAREER

Stress and negative emotions are common at work, but they can be managed effectively with the right strategies and practices. Some of the most effective stress-management techniques include deep breathing, progressive muscle relaxation, guided imagery, and mindfulness meditation.

These practices help us calm our nervous system, reduce stress hormones, and cultivate a sense of inner peace and well-being. They also help us develop greater self-awareness and emotional intelligence, enabling us to respond to challenging situations and difficult people with more patience, compassion, and wisdom.

In addition to these practices, it's also essential to develop healthy coping mechanisms for stress and negative emotions, such as journaling, talking to a friend or therapist, or engaging in creative or physical activities.

Embrace Mindfulness and Spiritual Practices

Finally, embracing mindfulness and spiritual practices can be a powerful way to find peace at work. Mindfulness means paying attention to the present moment, without judgment or distraction, and cultivating a sense of inner calm and awareness.

There are many ways to practice mindfulness at work, such as taking a few deep breaths before starting a task, taking short breaks to stretch or meditate, or practicing mindful listening and communication with colleagues and clients.

Spiritual practices, such as prayer, meditation, or yoga, can also be beneficial for finding peace at work. These practices help us connect with our deeper values and purpose, and cultivate a sense of inner peace and harmony. They also help us develop a more compassionate and empathic attitude towards ourselves and others, and increase our resilience and capacity for stress and uncertainty.

Conclusion

Finding peace at work is not always easy, but it's essential for our well-being and fulfillment. By developing a positive attitude and mindset, setting boundaries and prioritizing self-care, managing stress and emotions, and embracing mindfulness and spiritual practices, we can create a more fulfilling and joyful career, one that aligns with our values and purpose, and helps us achieve our goals and aspirations.

35: Overcoming Obstacles to Inner Peace: Dealing with Resistance and Challenges

Introduction

The journey towards inner peace is not always a smooth one. Along the way, we will encounter resistance and challenges that may test our commitment and determination to continue on this path. These obstacles can manifest in various forms such as self-doubt, negative thought patterns, stress, anxiety, and other emotional and psychological barriers. However, it is essential to remember that these obstacles are not roadblocks but opportunities for growth and transformation.

In this chapter, we will explore some of the common obstacles that may arise on our journey towards inner peace and provide practical strategies and techniques to overcome them.

Self-doubt and Negative Thought Patterns

One of the biggest obstacles to inner peace is self-doubt and negative thought patterns. These thought patterns can be so ingrained in our psyche that they become automatic, and we may not even be aware of them. They can prevent us from taking action towards our goals, limit our potential, and hold us back from experiencing inner peace.

To overcome self-doubt and negative thought patterns, we need to cultivate self-awareness and mindfulness. We must learn to recognize when these patterns arise and how they affect our thoughts, feelings, and behavior. We can use techniques such as journaling, meditation, and positive affirmations to reframe our thoughts and replace negative self-talk with positive and empowering messages.

Stress and Anxiety

Stress and anxiety are common obstacles that can hinder our progress towards inner peace. When we are stressed and anxious, our mind becomes overactive, and our thoughts become scattered, making it challenging to focus on the present moment.

To overcome stress and anxiety, we need to learn to manage our emotions effectively. We can use techniques such as deep breathing, progressive muscle relaxation, and mindfulness meditation to calm our minds and reduce stress levels. We can also incorporate physical exercise, healthy eating habits, and quality sleep into our daily routine to promote overall well-being.

External Circumstances

External circumstances such as financial difficulties, relationship problems, or health issues can be significant obstacles to inner peace. These circumstances can be overwhelming, and it may seem impossible to find peace amidst the chaos.

To overcome external obstacles, we need to focus on what we can control and let go of what we cannot control. We must learn to accept that life is unpredictable and that we cannot always have things our way. We can practice gratitude and focus on the positive aspects of our lives to cultivate a sense of inner peace amidst external challenges.

Resistance to Change

Resistance to change is a common obstacle to inner peace. It can be challenging to break out of our comfort zone and embrace new experiences and perspectives.

To overcome resistance to change, we must be willing to challenge our beliefs and assumptions. We can use techniques such as cognitive restructuring, exposure therapy, and visualization to reframe our thoughts and develop a more positive and open-minded attitude towards change.

Lack of Self-Care

Lack of self-care can also be an obstacle to inner peace. When we neglect our physical, emotional, and spiritual needs, we may feel depleted and overwhelmed.

To overcome the lack of self-care, we must prioritize our well-being and make self-care a non-negotiable part of our daily routine. We can practice self-compassion, set boundaries, and incorporate activities that nourish our mind, body, and spirit into our daily routine.

Conclusion

In conclusion, the journey towards inner peace is not always an easy one. However, with self-awareness, mindfulness, and effective strategies, we can overcome the obstacles that may arise along the way. By developing a sense of inner peace, we can cultivate a more fulfilling and joyful existence and live our lives to the fullest. Remember, the obstacles that we face are opportunities for growth and transformation.

36: Conclusion: Embracing Inner Peace for a Joyful and Fulfilling Existence

As we come to the end of this comprehensive guide to discovering the life-changing power of inner peace, it's time to reflect on what we've learned and how we can apply it to our daily lives.

Throughout this book, we've explored the negative effects of anxiety, stress, and negativity on our physical, emotional, and spiritual health. We've also discussed how cultivating inner peace through self-help strategies, mindfulness techniques, and spiritual practices can help us overcome these challenges and achieve a more fulfilling and joyful existence.

But what does it mean to embrace inner peace? And how can we make it a part of our daily lives? Let's delve deeper into these questions and explore some practical tips for cultivating inner peace.

First and foremost, embracing inner peace means letting go of the past and the future and living fully in the present moment. It means accepting things as they are and not letting our thoughts and emotions control us. This requires a conscious effort to become more mindful of our thoughts and feelings and to observe them without judgment.

One of the best ways to cultivate mindfulness is through meditation. Meditation involves focusing our attention on the present moment and letting go of distractions and negative thoughts. Regular meditation practice can help us reduce stress and anxiety, increase feelings of well-being, and improve our overall mental and physical health.

Another important aspect of embracing inner peace is developing self-awareness. This means becoming more aware of our thoughts, emotions, and behaviors and how they impact our lives and the lives of those around us. By developing self-awareness, we can identify negative patterns and beliefs and work to replace them with positive ones.

Self-care is also crucial for cultivating inner peace. This means taking care of our physical, emotional, and spiritual needs by getting enough sleep, eating a healthy diet, exercising regularly, spending time with loved ones, and engaging in activities that bring us joy and fulfillment. By prioritizing self-care, we can reduce stress and anxiety and improve our overall well-being.

In addition to self-help strategies and mindfulness techniques, spiritual practices can also help us cultivate inner peace. Whether it's through prayer, yoga, or other forms of spiritual practice, connecting with something greater than ourselves can provide a sense of purpose and meaning in our lives.

Ultimately, embracing inner peace requires a willingness to let go of negativity and cultivate positive habits and attitudes. It's a process that takes time and effort, but the rewards are well worth it. By embracing inner peace, we can live a more fulfilling and joyful existence and make a positive impact on the world around us.

In conclusion, I hope this guide has provided you with the tools and strategies you need to cultivate inner peace in your life. Remember that it's a journey, and it's okay to make mistakes along the way. Be kind to yourself, practice self-compassion, and keep moving forward. With patience, persistence, and a commitment to self-growth, you can embrace inner peace and live a life filled with joy and fulfillment.

Thank You

As we reach the end of this book, I want to say thanks for reading this book.

I want to get this information out to as many people as possible. If you found this book helpful, I would greatly appreciate you leaving me a review. This helps others find the book as well.

Disclaimer

This document is geared towards providing exact and reliable information in regards to the topic and issue covered. The publication is sold on the idea that the publisher is not required to render an accounting, officially permitted, or otherwise, qualified services. If advice is necessary, legal, financial, medical or professional, a practiced individual in the profession should be ordered.

This information is not presented by a financial or medical practitioner and is for entertainment, educational and informational purposes only. The content is not intended as a substitute for professional medical advice, diagnosis, or treatment. Always seek the advice of your physician or other qualified health care provider with any questions you may have regarding a medical condition. Never disregard professional medical advice or delay in seeking it because of something you have read.

The information provided herein is stated to be truthful and consistent, in that any liability, in terms of inattention or otherwise, by any usage or abuse of any policies, processes, or directions contained within is the solitary and utter responsibility of the recipient reader. Under no circumstances

DISCLAIMER

will any legal responsibility or blame be held against the publisher for any reparation, damages, or monetary loss due to the information herein, either directly or indirectly.